THRIFTY VEGAN

THRIFTY VEGAN

150 Budget-Friendly Recipes That Take Just 15 Minutes

Katy Beskow

Photography by Dan Jones

Hardie Grant

QUADRILLE

contents

introduction

It is hard to ignore the increasing costs of living, from food and energy prices, to everything in between. Tightening the food and grocery budget can seem like a reasonable way to help save money, but the practicalities of cooking with different ingredients and in new ways can seem daunting for any home cook.

In this book, I've chosen 150 of my favourite recipes from my best-selling *15 Minute Vegan* collection. These fail-safe recipes can be cooked in 15 minutes or less, use cost-effective cooking techniques, are easy to prepare, and use readily available ingredients that are budget-friendly.

One of the main tools in eating a balanced diet that doesn't cost the earth is choosing fresh produce that is in season. Not only is it cheaper to buy, but it tastes so much fresher, and has likely travelled fewer miles. Where you shop for your fresh produce can make a difference too, so consider switching to a local market, or another supermarket to save money. Alongside seasonal produce, I champion frozen vegetables and fruits as they are cost effective, low waste and require very little effort from you to prepare and cook. Canned pulses are a store-cupboard staple, meaning you'll always have tasty, protein-rich ingredients to cook with. They last for years in the cupboard, are easy to use and don't require hours of pre-soaking and boiling!

Not only do these recipes use good-value ingredients, but they all have a cooking time of just 15 minutes or less. With the ongoing rise in household energy bills, fast cooking is a great way to reduce your daily energy consumption, with simple and smart switches that mean you don't have to cook for hours to enjoy a delicious meal. The quick cooking times also mean that you'll be less likely to reach for that pricey takeaway menu – instead, you can have dinner ready in less time than it takes to order in.

There's a thrifty recipe for any time of the day; simply browse each chapter and see what takes your fancy:

Breakfast – a fresh and frugal way to start the day

Light bites – perfect for brunch, lunch or a light meal

Bigger things – family-friendly suppers that are quick and easy

Sweet stuff – desserts, bakes and treats for when you need something sweet

Essentials – dips, dressings, sauces and more

I've labelled the recipes that are suitable for freezing, so you can reduce food waste. Plus, these recipes are perfect for batch cooking, so you can get ahead.

Everyday vegan cooking can be cost efficient, quick and easy, whether you're cooking for yourself or for a larger family.

I hope this collection of recipes inspires you to think outside of the box, and get creative in the kitchen to create delicious and balanced meals, whatever your budget.

10 tips for smart shopping on a budget

Cooking delicious, fast, vegan food starts with having the right ingredients. Shopping on a budget doesn't have to be difficult; it just requires some preparation, knowing where to shop, and how to find the best quality ingredients for the lowest prices.

1) When meal planning, consider breakfast, lunch, dinner and snacks so you can stock up on the ingredients you need for trying new recipes, or creating your family favourites. It's also worth noting how many portions the recipe makes; if you make more than needed, don't forget to freeze the leftovers and you have a homemade ready meal available for another week's meal plan. The short investment of time it takes to create a weekly meal plan can really make financial savings. Think of a meal plan as a list of what you're going to cook and eat for the week – it's simple and effective.

2) Before writing a shopping list, take a look inside your refrigerator, freezer and cupboards. Note what you already have and think about how to use it while creating a meal plan for the week. For example, you may already have half a bag of onions from the week before, along with frozen peas and rice in the cupboard, so you've already got the basic ingredients for Kedgeree with paprika yogurt (page 45). This reduces waste and the cost of your food-shop bill.

3) Write a shopping list and stick to it! After creating your meal plan, you know exactly what you're going to cook and eat, with ingredients you already have available and what else you need to purchase. Mindfully purchase exactly what you need, and try not to go shopping on an empty stomach – you'll only be tempted into pricey extras that you haven't budgeted for.

4) Choose where is best to shop. Whether you prefer a large supermarket for its wide selection of products, a small supermarket due to close proximity, or online shopping for convenience, you'll find vegan items readily available. While larger, well-known stores may stock more choice of specialist vegan products, such as non-dairy cheeses, plant-based milks and vegan chocolates, budget chain supermarkets are certainly catching up with their selection. Veganism is now mainstream, and the availability of products is a reflection of this.

5) Consider shopping at fruit and vegetable markets for good prices on seasonal produce. Markets are often useful when buying products in bulk if you are batch-cooking or preparing meals for a family. Generally, the overheads of the market traders are less than supermarket chains, so savings can be passed on to the consumer. It's great to support local traders too.

6) When you're refilling the spice rack, take a look at the range and price of spices at Indian, Middle Eastern, Asian and Chinese shops and supermarkets. You'll be able to purchase more for your money! While you're there, check out the rice, egg-free noodles and coconut milk, as these items are often cheaper too.

7) When shopping in a large supermarket, look in the world-food aisle for store-cupboard essentials such as chickpeas, green lentils, coconut milk, tahini, soy sauce, rice and egg-free noodles. These staple ingredients are often remarkably cheaper in this aisle.

8) One certain way to reduce your food bill is to switch your branded products for supermarket own-brand alternatives. Supermarket 'value' ranges are another great switch, particularly for dried pasta and spaghetti, as these basic items are less likely to contain eggs in order to keep costs low (always check the ingredients). Challenge yourself and your family to determine if you can tell the difference between branded products and own-brand ones. Your wallet will thank you!

9) Reduced price, use-by-date, 'yellow sticker' items may seem like a bargain, but don't be tempted into buying something you won't eat just because it has been reduced to sell. If you make a purchase, eat or cook with it by the next day, or freeze it for use in the future (but don't forget it's in the freezer!). Similarly, be cautious of coupons and vouchers, and purchase only what you will actually use, no matter the discount.

10) Pre-prepared food isn't always bad, especially when cooking on a budget. For example, cooked beetroot (beet) that has been vacuum-packed is convenient and saves you a long cooking time at home. Chopped and frozen butternut squash, sweet potato, seasonal fruit and herbs are great buys to reduce preparation and cooking time, then you can use as much as you need before returning the rest to the freezer, resulting in no food waste.

what to buy

Cook up fast, delicious, and cost-effective vegan meals with the addition of a few staples to your store cupboard, refrigerator and freezer.

vegetables

Vegetables are the basis of a balanced vegan meal, so instead of thinking of vegetables as a side dish, make them the star of the show! Familiarize yourself with what vegetables are in season (there are multiple online resources) as you'll find them cheaper in shops and markets when there's an abundance, and they'll taste better too. Consider buying 'versatile vegetables', which can be used in varying ways – for example, spinach can be used in a curry or as a salad leaf, and broccoli can be stir-fried, quick-roasted or served as a crudité. Think about how you can finish the pack and write this into your weekly meal plan to avoid waste and save you money.

Prepared vegetables may set you back more money than their whole counterparts, so consider if it's worth it for the sake of a few moments' chopping. Some pre-prepared vegetables, such as vacuum-packed cooked beetroot (beet), save hours of roasting time and can be used instantly in a recipe, and don't cost remarkably more, so weigh up what works out as money-saving, time-saving and energy-saving for you. Frozen vegetables are a convenient way to use vegetables in your cooking for a low price with less waste, as you'll just use what you need and return the remainder to the freezer.

Peas, sweet potato, butternut squash, peppers and sweetcorn retain their flavour and texture when frozen, and are an economical and convenient addition to your kitchen. Some supermarkets and greengrocers offer excellent-value 'wonky vegetables', which contain non-standard shapes of popular veggies – who cares what shape the vegetables are when they are getting chopped up into a recipe? These are especially good for families, or if you are batch-cooking. If you're cooking for one, buy loose, unpackaged vegetables to give you the amount you need for a lower cost.

fruits

Not only do various fruits make an excellent addition to puddings, savoury dishes and salads, think about swapping your mid-morning or afternoon snack for a piece of fruit – you'll find it's a good saving compared to snacking on crisps or chocolate (and better for your health). Similarly to vegetables, enjoy fresh fruits seasonally for their best flavour and lowest price. Eating seasonally also enables you to try new fruits that perhaps are outside of what you would normally purchase. Soft fruits, such as berries and bananas, are versatile as a snack, to throw into a smoothie or use in a pudding, and they will cook in next to no time.

Canned fruits allow you to enjoy fruit that may be out of season, store for longer than fresh, and have the benefit of low or no cooking time. Frozen fruits are again excellent for enjoying fruits out of season, particularly when they will be cooked into a dessert or blended into a smoothie. Although you may not buy lemons and limes as an essential, they add an instant burst of flavour to any dish, with very little effort. Always choose unwaxed lemons and limes, as these fruits particularly can be coated with shellac, which is an animal ingredient, used to make the fruit appear shiny. For cheaper fruit, consider signing up to an allotment-share programme, or look into 'pick your own' days at local farms.

non-dairy milk, yogurt, cheese and butter

There is now a wide range of non-dairy milks available at supermarkets, including soya, oat, almond, cashew, coconut and rice milks. A few years ago, these were expensive to buy, but now the market has grown and prices are coming down. For the most cost-effective non-dairy milks, opt for a supermarket own-brand, and choose one that has been ultra-heat treated (UHT), meaning it does not need to be stored in a refrigerator until opened and has a long shelf life. It is worth trying a few non-dairy milks to find your favourite. I find the most versatile is unsweetened soya milk, as it can be used in hot drinks as well as savoury and sweet cooking.

Dairy-free yogurts can vary in price, often due to the added flavours, so buy a large pot of unsweetened soya yogurt and

simply add the flavour yourself, whether it is lemon or frozen fruits, or use the yogurt as a cooling dip for a savoury dish.

Most large supermarkets now stock a range of soft and hard vegan cheeses. The best-value vegan cheeses are often the supermarket own-brands, but shop around to find one you love. Vegan margarine (butter) is readily available in supermarkets. There's no need to spend a small fortune in health-food shops for any of these non-dairy items as they are widely available in supermarkets.

herbs and spices

Having a selection of herbs, spices and spice blends available in the kitchen means you can create exciting and delicious dishes using basic store-cupboard ingredients. Woody herbs such as rosemary, thyme, sage and oregano can give the flavour of a dish being slow-cooked for hours, when it's actually been cooked in just 15 minutes. These herbs are preserved well in dried form and are available at supermarkets in convenient jars. Leafy herbs such as flat-leaf parsley, coriander (cilantro), basil and mint may not be considered an essential on your shopping list when on a budget, but they lift a recipe with layers of freshness and flavour. These herbs are best used in fresh leaf form and can be kept fresher for longer when stored stem-down in a glass of water in a cool place. You could also consider growing herbs from a window box or small patch in the garden.

A few basic ground spices, such as cinnamon, ginger and turmeric, can be versatile in both sweet and savoury dishes. You may find these spices cheaper when bought in bulk or from Asian supermarkets. Store fresh ginger root in the freezer and grate from frozen into stir-fries and curries. Spice blends such as chilli powder, garam masala, Chinese five spice and jerk seasoning offer hits of flavour with very little preparation on your behalf, as the spices have been expertly blended. Add dried herbs and spices to your collection as you need them, and don't forget that they are a great gift to give and receive! Keep a small jar of curry paste in the refrigerator, ready to pack a flavour punch when you have little time to cook.

beans and pulses

Beans and pulses are a major source of protein in the vegan diet, and they just happen to be cheap, healthy and delicious too. Canned beans and pulses are cheap and widely available, and also don't require the long soaking and cooking time that they do when dried. Simply open the can, drain away the liquid, then thoroughly rinse them under cold running water to remove any 'canned' taste. Bulk buying of dried beans and pulses may be cheaper, but consider the gas or electric energy required to cook them. If this is a better option for you, consider batch-cooking the beans or pulses, then cool and freeze them in 400g (14oz) quantities, ready for quick recipes in the future. Have a selection of beans and pulses available, such as chickpeas, red kidney beans, butter (lima) beans and green lentils.

nuts and seeds

Nuts and seeds add instant texture, flavour and crunch to any dish, as well as being nutritious powerhouses of energy! Prices can vary, but they are cheaper when bought in a big pack in supermarkets. Broken, flaked, and non-standard shapes can be found cheaper, and they last for ages in the cupboard. Hazelnuts and sesame seeds are versatile for snacking and to use in recipes.

pasta

Most dried pasta bought in supermarkets is egg-free and vegan friendly, but always check the ingredients before buying. Pasta is cheap, fast to cook and easy to store in a cupboard, as well as being the basis for many lunches and dinners. If you have no preference about the shape of pasta, check out a supermarket's basic variety, as you can purchase a pack for a lower cost, including penne or fusilli, depending on the store.

rice

Not only is rice delicious and full of energy, it is an affordable ingredient to create a side dish, pilaf or pudding. Basmati, flaked, jasmine and American long grain have the shortest cooking times, whereas brown and wild rice take a little longer to cook. Tonnes of cooked rice are wasted every year; this can be down to overestimating volumes of uncooked rice – a good rule of thumb is to consider that the volume will double when cooked, and 80–90g (2¾–3¼oz) of uncooked rice will serve one person.

Often, people are afraid to eat leftover rice due to a bacterium that can develop; however, this risk is reduced if the rice is chilled quickly and refrigerated until used. It's safe to eat leftover rice that has been kept refrigerated within 24 hours, just ensure it is thoroughly reheated before eating.

oil

With a large selection of oils available, it can be hard to know which to buy and use for your cooking. Choose a mild-flavoured and cost-effective oil, such as sunflower or olive oil, for general cooking, and choose an extra virgin olive or cold-pressed rapeseed oil only for drizzling over finished dishes, when you want the peppery flavour of a more expensive oil. One general cooking oil, such as sunflower oil, and one oil for dressing, such as extra virgin olive oil, is sufficient for cooking on a budget.

salt

Salt is a natural flavour enhancer that, when used in moderation, lifts the taste of any dish. Opt for good-quality sea salt flakes that can be crushed gently between your fingers.

sugar

Enjoy the natural sweetness of sugar in puddings, and use it to take away the acidity of tomatoes in savoury dishes, but consume in moderation. Most sugar is vegan friendly as it is not combined with, or filtered through, animal products. Contact the supplier if you are unsure of the status of a brand.

canned chopped tomatoes and passata

Chopped tomatoes and smooth passata (strained tomatoes) are the basis for so many recipes, including casseroles, curries and pasta sauces. These items are cheap and have a long shelf life, as well as being easy to throw into a pan to create a hearty meal. Switch your usual brand to a supermarket basic and see if you can tell the difference in taste.

canned coconut milk

Where coconut milk is used in this book, it refers to the canned variety. It is thick, luxurious and silky when added to a soup, spiced dish or dessert. You can usually find the lowest-cost cans of coconut milk in the world-food aisle of supermarkets, or in Asian supermarkets. Full-fat varieties have the best flavour.

vegetable stock

Ensure vegetable stock cubes or bouillon are vegan, as they can often contain milk as a bulking agent. Use to add instant seasoning to soups and casseroles, or make your own by simmering peelings of vegetables and stalks of fresh herbs in water, then freezing into tubs for when you need to use it.

kitchen essentials

You don't need a large kitchen with an extensive array of gadgets in order to make fantastic, home-cooked meals. Add to your equipment collection over time, or as you can afford to do so.

A few good-quality knives will make food preparation much easier. Buy the best you can afford – you'll only need a small, medium and large knife, and a bread knife. Look for knives that are weighty, as these will reduce the effort needed when chopping. Look after your knives by chopping onto a wooden chopping board to absorb the impact. A food processor can chop vegetables in a matter of seconds, which is convenient and effortless, but can be a costly appliance to purchase.

Whip up silken soups, quick breadcrumbs and smooth houmous with a jug blender. For best results, choose a blender with over 1000W capabilities. A high-powered jug blender is an investment piece, but may be unaffordable or take up too much space in a small kitchen. Hand blenders are a good alternative, but may need a longer blending time and a little more effort.

One appliance that will save you money on food in the long run is a freezer. Use it to store frozen food essentials, including vegetables and fruits, as well as batch-cooked meals stored in airtight, labelled containers. Keep root ginger fresher for longer by storing it in the freezer and using it from frozen by grating it into your cooking. Can't think of a way to use up those fresh herbs? Chop the herbs and freeze them in ice-cube trays with water, then simply pop them into your next curry or casserole.

To cook in 15 minutes or less, choose pans that are silver or black inside, as they heat up quickly. You'll need a small, medium and large saucepan; a griddle pan; and a wok for its concave shape that quickly transfers heat to the food. Baking trays can be purchased cheaply in homeware shops and large supermarkets. Casserole dishes that are lined with a white inner are best saved for slow-cooked meals.

Make the most of your microwave by using it for more than just reheating. Cook basmati rice in just 10 minutes, steam fresh vegetables, or bake my Peanut butter melt-in-the-middle chocolate pudding (page 209). A microwave of 850W will heat your food evenly and quickly.

Slow cookers are an energy-efficient appliance, using less energy than a hob or oven. This hands-off approach to cooking technique takes over 4 hours, depending on the recipe.

A Y-peeler is a quick and efficient way to peel vegetables. Y-peelers are simple and comfortable to use, as well as taking off just the right amount of vegetable peel, leaving you with more vegetable to eat. Pick one up for under a fiver to make your preparation effortless.

reduce food waste in seven easy ways (and keep more money in your pocket!)

1) Store your ingredients in the correct place to extend their shelf life and preserve quality. Keep root vegetables and onions in a cool, dark place. Store leafy green vegetables, apples and grapes in the refrigerator between 1 and 4°C (34–39°F). Bread will become dry if stored in the refrigerator; however, if you plan on using it just for toast, it will certainly extend its life. Opened jars are best kept in a cool, dry place.

2) Before you start cooking, consider the quantity of ingredients you really need to use. An average portion size for uncooked rice is 80–90g (2¾–3¼oz) per person, and allow 80–100g (2¾–3½oz) dried pasta per person. Cooking a larger quantity than needed of these basic ingredients can be costly and wasteful. If you intentionally cook more than needed so you can save some for another time, make sure you plan when you are going to use it up – and stick to it!

3) Treat use-by dates on food labelling as guidelines and not rules. Imagine that your food doesn't have packaging or a use-by date. Use your senses to determine if it is edible and, of course, use your common sense. If a vegetable appears a little limp, it can be chopped up and used in a cooked dish, but if there is visible mould or an odour, it shouldn't be eaten for safety reasons.

4) Have a selection of stackable food storage boxes and labels to hand for storing leftovers. This will maximize the space in your freezer and allow you to recognize what is in each box (it's harder than you might think when a meal is frozen!). Keep leftovers of sauces in clean glass jars in the refrigerator, again to make them easy to recognize and locate, and to keep them fresher for longer.

5) Rotate the items in your refrigerator, freezer and cupboards to ensure that everything gets used before it passes its best quality and taste. This also reminds you of what you have available before you go shopping, so you can create meals around these products.

6) Make an informal list of the food you throw away, so you can recognize any patterns. Throwing away half a loaf of bread? Think about how better to store it and use it up. Throwing away that leftover pasta sauce you made last week? Remember to add leftovers to your meal plan. Throwing away an unopened bag of spinach? Base your shopping list around what you're actually going to cook that week.

7) Get creative with your leftover ingredients and cooked foods! Reducing waste and saving money on food bills doesn't have to be a struggle – there is a world of new recipes and meals available when you think outside of the box. Have fun with it!

BREAKFAST

cranberry and orange granola

Serves 2

This chewy granola tastes like it's been slow baked, although it's actually made in less than five minutes. Gently toasting the almonds and oats in a hot pan brings out all those slow-cooked flavours, while the maple syrup adds a smoky background taste. You'll never make granola the same way again.

1 tbsp blanched almonds

100g (3½oz/1 cup) rolled oats

1 tbsp coconut oil, at room temperature

2 tbsp maple syrup

1 tbsp dried cranberries

zest of 1 unwaxed orange

Toast the almonds and oats in a dry pan over a medium heat for 2 minutes, stirring frequently.

Spoon in the coconut oil, maple syrup, and dried cranberries and stir through to ensure all the oats are coated. Cook through for 2 minutes, stirring continuously, then grate over the orange zest.

Spoon the granola evenly onto a baking tray, allowing natural clumps of oats to form as they settle. Place the tray in the refrigerator for 10 minutes before serving.

Serve in a bowl with fresh fruit and soya yogurt.

TIP Pop the hot granola straight into the refrigerator for 10 minutes to cool and firm up if you want to eat it straight away. If you are blessed with more time, lay it out onto a baking sheet and allow it to cool to room temperature overnight.

cherry and garden mint smoothie bowl

Serves 2

Is there a prettier way to start your day than with this fresh and fruity smoothie bowl? This smoothie is so thick that you can eat it with a spoon and place toppings over it for added flavour, crunch and substance.

TIP Substitute frozen cherries for frozen blueberries, blackberries or strawberries, depending on the season.

200g (7oz/1¼ cups) frozen cherries

1 banana, roughly chopped

1 tbsp sweetened soya yogurt

Handful of fresh mint leaves

100ml (3½fl oz/scant ½ cup) almond milk

2 tbsp flaked (slivered) almonds

1 tbsp dried sour cherries

Add the frozen cherries, banana, soya yogurt, mint and almond milk to a blender and blend on high until completely smooth.

Pour into bowls and top with the flaked almonds and sour cherries.

cinnamon toast

Serves 4

Lazy mornings are made for sticky, messy breakfasts and sugary lips. Treat yourself to this sweet, French-style toast, with a coffee, perhaps over the morning newspapers.

———

TIP Get the oil nice and hot in a griddle pan as you make the batter so it will be ready to cook your cinnamon toast as soon as you are.

4 tbsp sunflower oil

200ml (7fl oz/scant 1 cup) soya milk

2 tbsp maple syrup

2 tsp vanilla extract

100g (3½oz/¾ cup) plain (all-purpose) flour

1¼ tsp ground cinnamon

4 slices of thick white bread

2 tbsp granulated sugar

Start by heating the sunflower oil in a griddle pan over a medium–high heat while you make the batter.

In a bowl, whisk together the soya milk, maple syrup and vanilla extract. Then stir in the flour and 1 teaspoon of the cinnamon. Mix together until it forms a smooth paste.

Dip a slice of bread into the batter to coat both sides. Use tongs to place the slice of bread onto the griddle pan, turning after 2 minutes when it is golden and crisp. Repeat with each slice of bread, keeping the others warm on top of each other on a plate lined with paper towels.

Mix the sugar and remaining cinnamon in a small bowl and sprinkle over each slice of toast before serving.

coffee and cream french toast

Serves 4

Serve this indulgent delight for breakfast, brunch or dessert (or any time in between).

TIP The batter can be made up to a day in advance and kept refrigerated until use. Perfect for effortless morning brunches!

4 tbsp sunflower oil

1 rounded tsp strong instant coffee granules

2 tsp boiling water

200ml (7fl oz/scant 1 cup) sweetened almond milk

2 tbsp maple syrup

1 tsp vanilla extract

100g (3½oz/¾ cup) plain (all-purpose) flour

4 slices of thick white bread

4 tsp caster (superfine) sugar

½ tsp ground cinnamon

½ tsp cocoa powder

4 scoops of vegan vanilla ice cream

Heat the oil in a griddle pan over a medium heat while you prepare the batter.

Add the coffee granules and boiling water to a large bowl to dissolve the grains. Pour in the almond milk, syrup, vanilla extract and flour, and use a balloon whisk to mix the batter until smooth.

Dip a slice of bread into the batter and coat on both sides, then use tongs to place on the hot griddle pan. Turn after 2 minutes and cook until golden and crisp. Repeat with each slice of bread, keeping the other slices warm on top of each other on a plate lined with paper towels to soak up excess oil. When all the bread has been grilled, arrange on plates.

Mix together the sugar, cinnamon and cocoa powder, and sprinkle over the toasts. Add a scoop of vanilla ice cream and serve.

three-ingredient banana pancakes

Makes about 9 small pancakes

These fluffy pancakes are my favourite way to start the day. The riper the banana, the sweeter the pancakes, so use up that banana you're ready to throw away. Serve with toasted pecan nuts, vegan yogurt and maple syrup if you happen to have some. Maple syrup can be expensive; however, you can buy premium-grade maple syrup from low-price supermarkets. It lasts for ages. If it is out of your price range, drizzle with golden syrup, or substitute for puréed seasonal soft fruits.

1 tbsp sunflower oil, for frying

1 ripe banana, peeled

100g (3½oz/1 cup) rolled oats

300ml (10½fl oz/1¼ cups) sweetened soya milk

Heat the sunflower oil in a frying pan over a low–medium heat while you prepare the pancake batter.

Throw the banana, oats and soya milk into a jug blender, or add the ingredients to a bowl and use a hand blender to blitz to a semi-smooth batter.

Add tablespoon-sized amounts of the batter to the hot pan, cook for 2 minutes until golden, then flip and cook the other side for a further 2 minutes. Serve hot.

TIP These pancakes work well with any type of non-dairy milk you have available. For a nuttier flavour, try almond milk.

sticky nutmeg and date palmiers

Serves 4

French-style patisserie will forever be known for being delicious, beautiful, and crafted by masters. These palmiers (or pig's ears as they are often called) are so easy to make with a simple roll-in technique. Most major brands of prepared puff pastry are made with oil instead of butter, but always check the ingredients before purchasing. Choose a variety that is pre-rolled to save time.

TIP Keep the puff pastry chilled until just before you use it so it doesn't become sticky or difficult to work with.

1 sheet of store-bought puff pastry (ensure dairy free)

1 tbsp caster (superfine) sugar

½ tsp grated nutmeg

4 pitted dates

1 tbsp soya milk, to glaze

Preheat the oven to 220°C/425°F/Gas 7.

Flatten the pastry sheet on a large board and evenly scatter with the sugar, then the nutmeg.

Chop the dates into small pieces and scatter them evenly over the pastry.

Fold each long side over to meet in the centre, then fold over once more to meet in the centre again.

Using a sharp knife, cut diagonal slices, about 2cm (¾in) thick. Arrange the slices cut-side down onto a baking tray, allowing for some spreading.

Brush over the soya milk and bake for 10 minutes until golden brown.

almond butter morning cookies

Makes 4 cookies

When the need for a breakfast cookie arises, these chewy little delights will come to the rescue. They are balanced enough to eat for breakfast, yet chocolatey enough to save for your 11am coffee. These cookies are packed with energy-giving nuts, oats, and, ahem, chocolate chips. Almond butter is readily available from health-food shops and large supermarkets, and is a welcome ingredient to any store cupboard.

TIP Switch almond butter for peanut butter, if you like.

3 tbsp almond butter

2 tbsp rolled oats

2 tbsp almond milk

1 tbsp dark (bittersweet) chocolate chips

1½ tbsp flaked (slivered) almonds

Preheat the oven to 200°C/400°F/Gas 6.

Spoon the almond butter, rolled oats and almond milk into a bowl and mix until well combined.

Stir in the chocolate chips and 1 tablespoon of the flaked almonds until a stiff dough forms.

Use your hands to roll out the dough into balls, then flatten onto a baking sheet.

Bake for 12 minutes, or until just golden. In the meantime, toast the remaining flaked almonds in a dry pan until they have just turned golden. The cookies are best eaten warm with a sprinkle of toasted almonds.

grilled grapefruit with maple syrup and pecans

Serves 2

Pink grapefruits are juicy, sweet and refreshing – perfect for breakfast with maple syrup and crunchy pecan nuts.

TIP It's easier and quicker to peel grapefruits when they are at room temperature.

2 pink grapefruits

4 tbsp maple syrup, plus an extra 4 tbsp for drizzling

½ tsp ground cinnamon

Handful of crushed pecans

Heat a griddle pan over a medium–high heat while you prepare the grapefruits.

Peel the grapefruits and cut them into 1cm (½in) slices. Remove any visible seeds.

Pour the maple syrup and cinnamon into a bowl and mix. Dip each grapefruit slice in the syrup, then use tongs to place on the griddle pan.

Cook for 30 seconds, then turn to cook the other side.

Transfer onto plates and drizzle with the extra maple syrup. Scatter over the pecans and enjoy hot.

pea guacamole toasts

Serves 2

Avocado toast makes for a delicious brunch, but let's face it, avocados are an expensive ingredient to purchase frequently. This guacamole uses frozen peas in place of avocado for a fresh, cost-effective brunch.

———

TIP I love a chunky guacamole, but if you prefer a smoother spread, simply blitz the peas in a blender before adding the other ingredients.

200g (7oz/1½ cups) frozen peas

1 small red onion, peeled and finely chopped

1 tomato, deseeded and chopped

Small handful of coriander (cilantro) leaves, finely chopped

Juice of 1 unwaxed lime

Generous pinch of sea salt flakes

2 slices of thick white toast

Defrost and simmer the peas in a saucepan of hot water for 2–3 minutes, then drain and tip the peas into a mixing bowl.

Use a potato masher to crush the peas until semi-smooth, then stir in the onion, tomato and coriander.

Stir in the lime juice and mix until combined. Season with sea salt and load generously onto hot toast.

breakfast rosti

Serves 2

I love serving these golden potato and spinach rosti for brunch, with herby mushrooms and tomatoes spooned over the top.

TIP There is no need to peel the potatoes, as the skins add extra flavour to the rosti.

2 large baking potatoes, thoroughly washed

2 handfuls of spinach leaves

Pinch of nutmeg

Generous pinch of sea salt flakes and freshly ground black pepper

4 tbsp sunflower oil

8 closed-cup mushrooms, roughly sliced

5 cherry tomatoes, halved

½ tsp dried oregano

Grate the potatoes onto a clean, dry dish towel, then squeeze out as much moisture as possible. Put the dry, grated potato into a bowl, then mix in the spinach leaves and nutmeg. Season with sea salt flakes and black pepper.

Heat 3 tablespoons of the oil in a large frying pan over a high heat. Squeeze the grated potato together, shaping it into two dense masses. Carefully place into the hot frying pan and flatten with a spatula.

Fry for 5 minutes until golden, then flip and fry for 5 minutes on the other side.

In the meantime, heat the remaining tablespoon of oil in a separate frying pan over a medium heat and cook the mushrooms, cherry tomatoes and oregano for 5–6 minutes until softened.

Carefully remove the rosti from the pan and place on serving plates. Spoon over the herby mushrooms and tomatoes. Serve hot.

edamame beans on toast with lemon and chives

Serves 2

Garlic, lemon and chives season edamame beans beautifully in this modern twist on a breakfast classic.

TIP Frozen edamame beans are available from many large supermarkets. They are very versatile, so keep a handy bag in the freezer.

1 tbsp olive oil

6 tbsp edamame (soya) beans

1 clove of garlic, crushed

Juice of 1 unwaxed lemon

Small handful of chives, finely chopped

Pinch of coarse sea salt

2 thick slices of sourdough

Drizzle of extra virgin olive oil (optional)

4 cherry tomatoes, quartered

In a pan, heat the olive oil and edamame beans over a high heat for 2 minutes. Add the garlic to the pan and quickly stir-fry for another minute.

Reduce the heat to medium-low. Add the lemon juice to the pan. Stir the chives through the beans along with the salt. Cook for a further minute and then smash the beans roughly.

Lightly toast the bread until crisp and golden. Pile the beans high on the bread and drizzle with extra virgin olive oil for an added fruity flavour, if desired. Top with the tomatoes and serve.

tomato-stuffed field mushrooms

Serves 2

I love these herby mushrooms served over thick slices of toast for brunch. They also make the perfect addition to any pasta dish later in the day.

———

TIP Preheat the oven as you prepare the mushrooms to ensure optimum cooking quality.

4 large field mushrooms

12–16 cherry tomatoes

2 tbsp olive oil

Pinch of dried thyme

Pinch of dried oregano

Pinch of sea salt

Preheat the oven to 200°C/400°F/Gas 6.

Remove the stems of the mushrooms and discard. Arrange the mushrooms on a baking tray, flat-side up, and fill with the cherry tomatoes.

Drizzle with the oil and sprinkle with the thyme and oregano. Bake for 13–14 minutes until tender.

Season with sea salt just before serving.

breakfast burritos

Serves 2

Burritos make the best
on-the-go breakfasts.
Simply wrap them up
in some kitchen foil to
keep them hot!

———————

TIP If you don't have fresh chillies
available, use a pinch of dried
chilli flakes and an extra squeeze
of juice from an unwaxed lime.

1 tbsp sunflower oil

*1 red (bell) pepper, sliced
into strips*

*2 spring onions (scallions),
roughly chopped*

*235g (8oz) can cannellini
beans, drained and rinsed*

1 tsp mild chilli powder

1 tsp smoked paprika

Pinch of ground cumin

Juice of 1 unwaxed lime

*Handful of fresh coriander
(cilantro), roughly torn, plus
extra to garnish*

*1 red chilli, deseeded and
finely sliced*

1 large avocado, finely sliced

4 soft tortilla wraps

*Pinch of sea salt flakes and
freshly ground black pepper*

In a large frying pan or wok,
heat the oil over a high heat.

Add the red pepper and spring
onions to the pan and cook for
1–2 minutes.

Add the cannellini beans to
the pan along with the chilli
powder, smoked paprika and
cumin. Season with sea salt
flakes and black pepper. Stir
frequently, crushing the beans
slightly, cooking for 2 minutes
more.

Remove the pan from the
heat and stir through the lime
juice, coriander and red chilli.

Lay out the wraps and load
in the hot filling. Top with
avocado slices and scatter
with coriander to garnish.
Fold in both ends and then
roll up – secure with foil.

kedgeree with paprika yogurt

Serves 2 generously

Perfect for breakfast, brunch, lunch or dinner, this kedgeree has plenty of dill and lemon and is great served hot with cooling salted yogurt and paprika. A nicely balanced dish that everyone will love.

TIP I love adding green vegetables to the rice, including broccoli, green beans and peas, but other quick-cook vegetables work well, including courgettes (zucchini), spinach and broad (fava) beans. Work with what you've got!

1 tbsp sunflower oil

1 onion, peeled and finely chopped

1 clove of garlic, peeled and crushed

1 tsp mild curry powder

½ tsp ground turmeric

½ tsp ground cumin

150g (5½oz/¾ cup) basmati rice

700ml (1¼ pints/3 cups) hot water

8 small florets of broccoli

8 green beans, halved

2 tbsp frozen peas

Handful of dill, finely chopped

Juice of ½ unwaxed lemon

2 tbsp unsweetened soya yogurt

Pinch of fine sea salt

Sprinkle of smoked paprika

Heat the oil in a large saucepan over a medium–high heat and cook the onion and garlic for 2 minutes. Spoon in the curry powder, turmeric and cumin and cook for a further minute.

Stir through the rice and pour in 500ml (17½fl oz/2 cups) of the hot water. Simmer for 5 minutes, stirring frequently.

Add the broccoli and beans and pour in the remaining 200ml (7fl oz/scant 1 cup) of water, then cook for a further 4 minutes until the water has absorbed into the rice. Stir through the peas and cook for a further minute.

Remove from the heat and stir through the dill. Squeeze over the lemon juice and divide into two bowls.

Add 1 tablespoon of soya yogurt over the kedgeree in each bowl and season with fine sea salt. Sprinkle a little smoked paprika over the yogurt and serve.

carrot and ginger zinger

Serves 2

A freshly pressed juice is the perfect accompaniment to any breakfast. I love this one because it uses up what's left at the back of the refrigerator – waste not, want not!

TIP The most time-consuming part of making a fresh juice is cleaning the juicer afterwards. So, make double the quantity, pour into an airtight jar and store in the refrigerator for up to 3 days.

4 carrots, washed and chilled

2 red apples (stems and pips removed if your home juicer requires)

2cm (¾in) piece of ginger, peeled

4 ice cubes (optional)

Run the carrots, apples and ginger through a juicer.

Serve in glasses over ice, if you like.

LIGHT
BITES

tempura vegetables with a soy, chilli and coriander dipping sauce

Serves 4

People often consider tempura a difficult dish to create; however, it is in fact incredibly easy, with just a few simple ingredients required. The trick to creating the perfect light yet crispy batter is using sparkling, carbonated water that is ice cold. Use vegetables that need minimal preparation, such as button mushrooms and broccoli, to save time.

TIP The dipping sauce can be made in advance and refrigerated in a sealed container for up to 3 days.

200ml (7fl oz/scant 1 cup) sunflower oil, for frying

For the vegetables

8 spears of long-stem broccoli, any woody stems trimmed

8 baby carrots

8 radishes, any stringy roots removed

12 button mushrooms, brushed clean

For the batter

150g (5½oz/generous 1 cup) plain (all-purpose) flour

100g (3½oz/generous ¾ cup) cornflour (cornstarch)

1 tsp baking powder

200ml (7fl oz/scant 1 cup) ice-cold sparkling water

For the soy, chilli and coriander dipping sauce

200g (7oz/¾ cup) passata (strained tomatoes)

2 tbsp soy sauce

1 tbsp maple syrup

Pinch of dried chilli flakes (red pepper flakes)

Handful of fresh coriander (cilantro), finely chopped

1 lime

Heat the oil in a deep pan over a high heat while you prepare the vegetables.

Now make the batter. In a wide bowl, mix together the flour, cornflour and baking powder before whisking in the ice-cold sparkling water. Whisk gently until just smooth. Dip in the vegetables and ensure they are evenly coated in batter, shaking off any excess.

Using a slotted spoon, carefully add half the vegetables to the hot oil and cook for 2–3 minutes. Try not to overfill the pan with the vegetables, as they will stick together. When the batter has puffed up, carefully remove the tempura from the pan and drain on paper towels, then add the rest of the vegetables to the pan, again cooking for 2–3 minutes.

In the meantime, make the dipping sauce. Pour the passata, soy sauce, maple syrup, chilli flakes and coriander into a bowl. Cut the lime in half and squeeze in the juice through a sieve to stop any pips going into the bowl. Whisk until combined.

Serve the tempura immediately with individual bowls of the dipping sauce.

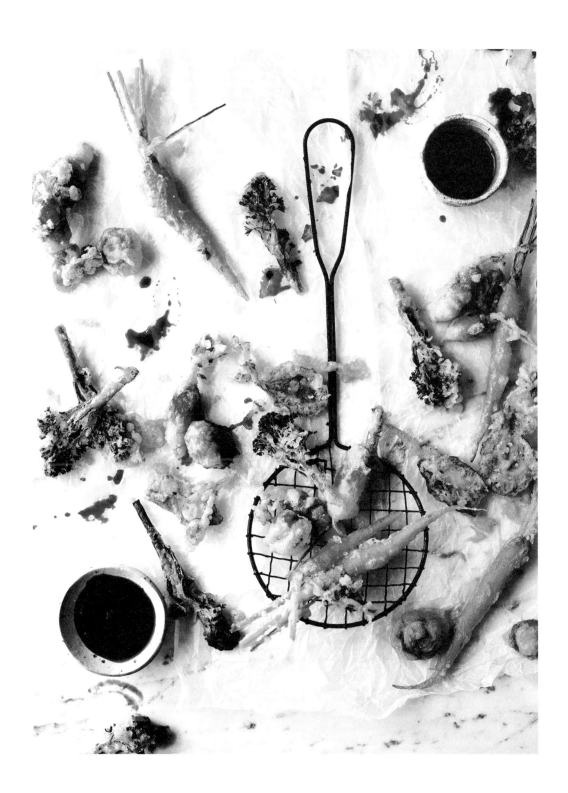

speedy samosas

Serves 2

This recipe was born when I had a craving for samosas, but not enough time to make them. These speedy samosas have all of the flavours you're familiar with, but use soft tortillas as the wrapping. Samosas in under 15 minutes? You'll be hooked.

TIP Garam masala is a pre-mixed Indian spice blend, so keep a jar in the cupboard to save you time blending spices.

1 tbsp sunflower oil, plus 2 tsp for brushing and sealing

1 small red onion, finely chopped

8 green beans, finely chopped

1 tbsp frozen peas

1 carrot, grated

2 tsp garam masala

Juice of 1 unwaxed lemon

2 soft tortillas

Preheat the oven to 200°C/400°F/Gas 6.

Heat the 1 tablespoon of sunflower oil in a frying pan over a medium–high heat and soften the red onion for 1–2 minutes. Throw in the green beans, peas and carrot, and cook for a further 3 minutes, stirring frequently until the vegetables have started to soften. Sprinkle in the garam masala, stir through to coat the vegetables and cook for a further minute. Squeeze in the lemon juice and stir.

Cut the tortillas in half. Place one-quarter of the filling in the middle of each tortilla half, then fold in both sides to create a triangle. You're essentially folding the tortilla into thirds over the filling. Use a pastry brush to apply a little sunflower oil along the inside edges of the samosas, then push to seal them. Brush a little oil over the top of the samosas too. Bake for 5–6 minutes until golden. Serve hot or cold.

carrot and onion bhajis

Makes about 8

My favourite Indian snacks are onion bhajis – not the type that come from a packet in the supermarket, but the aromatic, straight-out-of-hot-oil kind. I love using up unloved carrots in this recipe, even those slightly limp ones that live at the back of the vegetable drawer.

1 medium carrot, peeled and grated

1 onion, peeled and finely sliced

1 tsp cumin seeds

1 tsp garam masala

½ tsp mild chilli powder

1 tsp fine sea salt

5 tbsp plain (all-purpose) flour

500ml (17½fl oz/2 cups) sunflower oil, for frying

Juice of ½ unwaxed lemon

Combine the carrot and onion in a bowl, then stir through the cumin seeds, garam masala, chilli powder, salt and flour.

Mix in 50ml (1¾fl oz/scant ¼ cup) of cold water to form a thick batter.

Heat the oil in a deep saucepan until hot (test this by dropping a small amount of batter into the oil; it should sizzle, rise and become golden), then carefully spoon tablespoon-sized portions of batter into the oil. Cook for 4–5 minutes until golden, then carefully remove with a slotted spoon and drain on paper towels.

Squeeze over the lemon juice and serve hot with sauces of your choice.

TIP Cook 3–4 bhajis at a time to ensure they don't stick to each other in the pan.

loaded tortilla chips with lime yogurt

Serves 2

A mountain of hot, crisp tortilla chips, feisty red chillies and cooling lime-infused yogurt make for the perfect comfort food – they are almost too good to share!

———

TIP Serve as a side to the Chocolate chilli (page 166), or enjoy as a snack.

2 soft tortillas, cut into rough triangles

½ tsp dried chilli flakes (red pepper flakes)

Drizzle of sunflower oil

1 red chilli, deseeded and finely sliced

1 spring onion (scallion), finely sliced

Small handful of fresh coriander (cilantro), roughly chopped

Generous pinch of smoked sea salt

1 small avocado, peeled and finely sliced

2 tbsp unsweetened soya yogurt

Zest of 1 unwaxed lime

Preheat the oven to 200°C/400°F/Gas 6.

Arrange the tortilla triangles on a baking tray and scatter with the chilli flakes. Drizzle with sunflower oil and rub the oil over the triangles to evenly coat. Bake for 8 minutes until golden and crisp, then carefully place the hot chips onto a platter.

Sprinkle over the red chilli, spring onion, coriander and smoked sea salt, then add the avocado slices.

Spoon on the soya yogurt and sprinkle the lime zest over the top.

black pepper courgette fries

Serves 1

Courgettes will become your new best friend after you've tried this simple recipe. The fries are brilliant served with Moroccan-style flatbread pizza (page 118).

———

TIP For a lighter batter, use 50ml (1¾fl oz) chilled sparkling water instead of still water.

1 rounded tbsp plain (all-purpose) flour

1 tsp freshly ground black pepper, for the batter, plus extra to season

300ml (10½fl oz/1¼ cups) sunflower oil, for frying

1 medium courgette (zucchini), sliced into fries

Generous pinch of sea salt flakes, crushed

Mix the flour with 50ml (1¾fl oz/scant ¼ cup) of cold water until you form a batter the consistency of double cream. Stir through the teaspoon of black pepper.

Heat the sunflower oil in a heavy-bottomed saucepan to 180°C (350°F), or until a small piece of courgette browns and rises to the surface when dropped in.

Dip each of the courgette fries into the batter, then carefully place in the oil, being careful not to overfill the pan. Fry for 3–4 minutes until golden and crisp.

Use a slotted spoon to remove the fries from the pan and drain on paper towels. Season with sea salt and extra black pepper to taste.

patatas bravas

Serves 4

This Spanish tapas dish is the perfect way to revive leftover potatoes and create a small sharing plate. Serve alongside Gigantes plaki (page 108) and some nice crusty bread.

TIP If you don't have any leftover boiled potatoes, canned new potatoes work well in this recipe. Simply drain and rinse them thoroughly, so the flavours absorb into the potatoes.

Suitable for freezing.

3 tbsp sunflower oil

1 red onion, peeled and finely chopped

3 cloves of garlic, peeled and crushed

2 tsp sweet paprika

1 tsp smoked paprika

1 tsp mild chilli powder

400g (14oz) can chopped tomatoes

½ tsp sugar

300g (10½oz) leftover boiled potatoes, cut into small cubes

Generous pinch of sea salt flakes

Handful of flat-leaf parsley, roughly chopped

1 red chilli, deseeded and finely sliced

Heat 1 tablespoon of the sunflower oil in a frying pan over a medium–high heat and cook the onion for 2 minutes until softened. Add the garlic, both paprikas and the chilli powder, stir, and cook for a further minute.

Tip in the chopped tomatoes and sugar, reduce to a medium heat, and cook for 10 minutes, stirring occasionally.

In the meantime, heat the remaining 2 tablespoons of oil in a separate frying pan over a medium heat and fry the potato cubes for 10 minutes, or until the edges are golden.

Stir the golden potatoes into the spicy tomato sauce. Remove from the heat, then season with sea salt.

Scatter over the parsley and chilli slices just before serving.

spiced flatbreads

Serves 4

Don't waste money on flavoured flatbreads. Use store-cupboard spices to liven up plain flatbreads with this Middle Eastern-inspired flavour infusion. Enjoy with the Spinach, chickpea and lemon pilaf (page 96).

———

TIP This recipes also works well with pita breads, so use what you have to hand!

2 tbsp olive oil

¼ tsp ground cumin

¼ tsp ground ginger

¼ tsp ground allspice

¼ tsp mild chilli powder

Zest of 1 unwaxed lemon

4 large flatbreads (ensure dairy free)

1 tbsp sultanas (golden raisins)

Small handful of flat-leaf parsley leaves, roughly chopped

Pinch of sea salt flakes

Preheat the oven to 180°C/350°F/Gas 4.

In a small bowl, mix together the oil, cumin, ginger, allspice, chilli powder and lemon zest until combined.

Arrange the flatbreads on a baking tray. Brush over a thin coat of the spiced oil using a pastry brush, then sprinkle over the sultanas.

Bake for 8–10 minutes until hot and golden, then scatter with the parsley and sea salt.

giant spring rolls

Serves 4

I'm sure I don't speak for just myself when I say that I want more than a bite-size spring roll. These large rolls are baked until they are crispy and golden, and are filled with hot, fragrant vegetables. Serve with a bowl of Sweet chilli sauce (page 301) for dipping.

TIP Stir-fried radishes have a similar crunch to water chestnuts, but are much cheaper to buy.

1 tbsp sunflower oil

2 carrots, peeled and shaved into ribbons using a vegetable peeler

8 florets of long-stem broccoli, tough ends discarded

4 radishes, finely sliced

2 spring onions (scallions), roughly chopped

¼ savoy cabbage, finely sliced

1 tsp Chinese five spice

1 tbsp light soy sauce

8 tortilla wraps

1 tsp sesame seeds

Sweet chilli sauce (page 301), to serve

Preheat the oven to 220°C/425°F/Gas 7.

Heat ½ tablespoon of the oil in a wok over a high heat and stir-fry the carrots, broccoli, radishes, spring onions and cabbage for 1 minute. Spoon in the Chinese five spice and soy sauce and stir-fry for a further minute.

Place a tortilla wrap on a flat surface and spoon in ⅛ of the hot vegetable mixture on the right side of the wrap. Fold the bottom and top in towards the centre approximately 3cm (1¼in), then roll tightly from the right side to the left, rolling until it looks like a closed burrito. Repeat for the remaining giant spring rolls.

Place the rolls on a baking tray, then use a pastry brush to brush the remaining oil over the top and sides of the rolls. Sprinkle with the sesame seeds.

Bake for 10–12 minutes until the rolls are golden and crisp.

Serve with the sweet chilli dipping sauce.

edamame, lime and sesame jar salad

Serves 1

This is a make-now-and-enjoy-later salad that looks as pretty as it tastes, combining flavours of edamame, coriander and lime for a refreshing lunch.

——————

TIP Glass jars are great for storing and transporting salads and snacks, perfect to store your made-in-advance creations. They're reusable and they look great too!

2 tbsp frozen edamame (soya) beans

1 carrot, grated

Small handful of fresh coriander (cilantro)

5cm (2in) piece of cucumber, finely sliced

6 cherry tomatoes, halved

1 avocado

Juice of 1 unwaxed lime

Small handful of baby spinach leaves

1 tsp sesame seeds

Add the edamame beans to a pan and pour over boiling water. Cook over a high heat for 4 minutes, then drain. Rinse in cold water to cool them down.

Add the carrot to the jar as a base layer and sprinkle over the coriander.

Add the cucumber next, then the tomatoes.

Spoon in the edamame beans and press them down gently.

Halve the avocado, remove the stone and peel. Finely chop the flesh and add it to the jar. Squeeze over the lime juice.

Top with the spinach leaves – adding them last ensures they will stay crisp, away from the moisture from the other vegetables. Sprinkle with the sesame seeds and place the lid on the jar. Refrigerate until you wish to eat the salad, then simply shake the jar to coat the salad in the lime juice.

squash and orange salad with hazelnuts

Serves 2

This salad will keep you warm in cooler months, with fiery ginger, sweet squash and crunchy hazelnuts.

TIP Blast the butternut squash in a microwave for 2–3 minutes to soften the skin and make peeling and chopping easy and fast.

2 tbsp sunflower oil

½ butternut squash, peeled and chopped into small, even chunks

1 courgette (zucchini)

1cm (½in) piece of ginger, peeled and grated

100g (3½oz) sugar snap peas

1 avocado, peeled and chopped

Handful of fresh coriander (cilantro), roughly chopped

2 generous handfuls of watercress

Handful of hazelnuts

For the dressing

4 tbsp extra virgin olive oil

1 unwaxed orange

1 tsp wholegrain mustard

Heat the oil in a large wok over a medium–high heat. Add the butternut squash to the wok and cook for 5 minutes.

In the meantime, peel the courgette into strips using a vegetable peeler. Add it to the pan with the ginger and sugar snap peas and cook for a further 5 minutes, stirring frequently to avoid burning.

While the vegetables are cooking, arrange the avocado and coriander on a large plate with the watercress and hazelnuts.

To make the dressing, add the oil to a bowl, then slice the orange in half and squeeze in the juice through a sieve. Whisk in the mustard until fully combined.

Place the hot vegetables over the watercress salad and drizzle over the dressing. Serve hot.

fennel and radicchio slaw

Serves 2

This fresh, fragrant, sweet and bitter slaw is the perfect side to the rich Chestnut mushroom bourguignon (page 174). It's simple to make, yet the flavours are complex enough to get everyone talking!

TIP This slaw will keep for 2–3 days in an airtight container in the refrigerator.

1 head of fennel, finely sliced

1 head of radicchio, finely sliced

Zest and juice of 1 unwaxed orange

Generous drizzle of smoked extra virgin rapeseed oil

Generous pinch of smoked sea salt flakes, crushed

Mix together the fennel and radicchio in a bowl.

Grate in the orange zest and squeeze over the orange juice, then stir through to combine.

Finish with a drizzle of smoked rapeseed oil and a sprinkle of smoked sea salt.

grilled peach, basil and walnut salad

Serves 2

There's something beautiful about hot, caramelized peaches placed over fragrant basil that makes this more than just a salad. Team with hot, toasted walnuts for added bite.

───────

TIP The slight bitterness of rapeseed oil works perfectly drizzled over this salad.

4 ripe peaches, halved and stones removed

2 generous handfuls of watercress

2 handfuls of lamb's lettuce (mâche)

30g (1oz) fresh basil leaves

2 tbsp walnut pieces

Drizzle of extra virgin rapeseed oil

Pinch of freshly ground black pepper

Heat a griddle pan over a high heat. Place the peaches cut-side down and cook for 4–5 minutes until caramelized with grill marks.

In the meantime, arrange the watercress, lamb's lettuce and basil over a serving plate.

Place the hot peaches over the leaves while you carefully toast the walnuts in the pan for 30 seconds, then sprinkle them over the salad.

Drizzle with the rapeseed oil, then season with black pepper and serve.

panzanella

Serves 2

A delicious and rustic salad to use up stale bread. I love to use leftover crusty white bread, but thick-sliced or ciabatta is also delicious.

TIP Good-quality extra virgin olive oil gives a fruity, peppery taste to this salad. Choose the best you can afford, and save it for drizzling and dressing.

200g (7oz) day-old white bread, torn into 4cm (1½in) pieces

400g (14oz) mixed tomatoes, roughly chopped

Generous pinch of sea salt flakes

Generous pinch of freshly ground black pepper

6 tbsp extra virgin olive oil

4 sundried tomatoes in oil, roughly chopped

2 tbsp capers, drained

Generous handful of basil leaves, torn

Preheat the oven to 160°C/315°F/Gas 2–3.

Arrange the torn bread on a baking tray, then dry out in the oven for 12 minutes.

In a bowl, season the tomatoes with the sea salt and black pepper, then drizzle with the oil. Stir through the sundried tomatoes and capers, then leave to infuse for 10 minutes.

Stir the warm bread into the tomato mixture and scatter over the basil leaves to serve.

thai-style slaw

Serves 4

Give your classic coleslaw a nutty twist. Store-cupboard ingredients make a no-cook sauce, which is great with crunchy, raw vegetables. Delicious served with Roasted broccoli curry (page 153).

TIP The oil content in peanut butter varies from brand to brand, so you may need to add a little more water to the sauce. Add it 1 tablespoon at a time, until the sauce evenly coats the back of the spoon.

4 tbsp smooth peanut butter

1 tbsp dark soy sauce

1 red chilli, deseeded and finely chopped

1 spring onion (scallion), finely sliced

2 carrots, peeled and finely sliced

1 red (bell) pepper, deseeded and finely sliced

1 red onion, peeled and finely sliced

1 green apple, cored and finely sliced

¼ small red cabbage, finely shredded

Handful of fresh coriander (cilantro), roughly chopped

In a mixing bowl, whisk together the peanut butter and soy sauce with 100ml (3½fl oz/scant ½ cup) of cold water until smooth. Stir through the chilli and spring onion.

In a serving bowl, toss together the carrots, red pepper, onion, green apple, cabbage and coriander.

Pour over the peanut sauce and stir until the vegetables are evenly coated.

citrus fregola salad

Serves 2

This zesty, fresh and fragrant salad makes the perfect garden lunch on a summer's day. Fregola is small, pea-shaped pasta, which cooks into soft little cushions. If you don't have fregola in the cupboard, giant couscous is an excellent substitute.

───────

TIP Use the zest of an unwaxed lime in this salad, then use the juice to make Caribbean-style sweet potato and coconut soup (page 103).

200g (7oz) fregola pasta (ensure egg free)

1 orange, peeled and sliced into rounds

1 grapefruit, peeled and sliced into rounds

Zest of 1 unwaxed lime

2 generous handfuls of watercress

Handful of basil leaves

Juice of 1 unwaxed lemon

Drizzle of extra virgin olive oil

Generous pinch of sea salt flakes

Bring a saucepan of water to the boil and tip in the fregola. Simmer over a medium heat for 10 minutes until al dente.

In the meantime, add the orange and grapefruit slices to a bowl, then sprinkle over the lime zest. Mix in the watercress and basil, and leave to infuse.

Drain the water from the fregola and toss the fregola into the orange salad. Squeeze over the lemon juice and drizzle with extra virgin olive oil, then stir to combine.

Season with sea salt flakes and serve while the fregola is hot.

carrot, mango and red onion ribbon salad

Serves 2

If you're looking for a colourful side to liven up a meal, simply throw together these ingredients to create a pretty, vibrant salad. It's deliciously fresh with Tea-infused chana masala (page 161).

———

TIP A good quality Y-shaped vegetable peeler works best to create the carrot ribbons. A great addition to your kitchen at a nominal cost.

2 red onions, peeled and finely sliced

4 large carrots, peeled and shaved into ribbons using a vegetable peeler

1 mango, peeled, pitted and finely sliced

Generous handful of flat-leaf parsley, finely chopped

Juice of 1 unwaxed lime

Generous pinch of sea salt flakes

Place the red onions in a heatproof bowl and pour over enough boiling water to cover. Allow to stand for 5 minutes to take away the acidity of the onions.

In the meantime, toss together the carrots and mango.

Drain away the water from the red onions, then rinse in cold water and pat dry. Toss the onions with the carrots and mango.

Stir through the parsley and lime juice. Season well with sea salt flakes.

stir-fried beetroot, ginger and lemon

Serves 2 generously

This may be your easiest stir-fry recipe yet! Pre-cooked beetroot is available in supermarkets for a great price, and tastes vibrant with chilli, ginger, lemon and parsley. I make this when I have leftover rice, but you can simply cook some dried rice for 10 minutes while preparing the fresh ingredients. Pre-cooked pouch rice can be pricey, but it is convenient, so if you're in a rush, look out for special offers in supermarkets.

1 tbsp sunflower oil

1 tsp dried chilli flakes (red pepper flakes)

3cm (1¼in) piece of ginger, peeled and grated

1 clove of garlic, peeled and finely sliced

4 leaves of cavolo nero, stems discarded and roughly sliced

300g (10½oz) vacuum-packed cooked beetroot (beet), drained and roughly sliced

200g (7oz/1½ cups) cooked or leftover rice

Juice of ½ unwaxed lemon

Handful of flat-leaf parsley, roughly chopped

Pinch of sea salt flakes

Heat the oil in a wok over a high heat and cook the chilli flakes, ginger and garlic for 1 minute to infuse the oil.

Throw in the cavolo nero and stir-fry for 2 minutes.

Add the beetroot and cooked rice. Stir-fry for a further minute, ensuring the beetroot keeps its firmness and shape.

Remove from the heat and squeeze over the lemon juice, then stir in the parsley. Season with sea salt flakes.

TIP Sliced kale or savoy cabbage makes a great substitute for cavolo nero in this stir-fry.

satay noodles

Serves 2

If you're a lover of peanut butter, this bowl of creamy noodles is designed for you. With the perfect balance of heat, salt and bitters, you'll have this on your table before you can run out to grab a hot box!

TIP This versatile sauce can also be used as a stir-fry sauce or creamy dipping sauce.

For the sauce

4 tbsp smooth peanut butter

2 tsp dark soy sauce

Generous pinch of dried chilli flakes

Juice of 1 unwaxed lime

For the noodles

1 tbsp sunflower oil

Handful of sugar snap peas, halved

1 small carrot, finely sliced

2 spring onions (scallions), chopped

2 packs of soft ready-to-wok noodles (egg free)

2 tsp white sesame seeds

Small handful of fresh coriander (cilantro)

1 red chilli, deseeded and finely sliced

To make the sauce, whisk together the peanut butter, soy sauce and chilli flakes along with 200ml (7fl oz/ scant 1 cup) cold water in a bowl. Whisk in the lime juice to form a smooth paste.

For the noodles, heat the oil in a wok over a high heat. When the oil is hot, throw in the vegetables and stir-fry for 1–2 minutes. Separate the soft noodles and add them to the wok. Pour in the peanut sauce and stir-fry for a further minute.

Sprinkle over the sesame seeds, coriander and fresh chilli. Serve immediately.

cashew chow mein

Serves 1

Before you order that takeaway for one, consider this store-cupboard chow mein, ready in under 10 minutes with minimal preparation. It will become your go-to 'fakeaway' dish.

TIP Long-stem broccoli requires minimal preparation, as all of the vegetable can be eaten. If you don't have it available, use regular broccoli, with the tough stem trimmed, or switch for a handful of sugar snap peas.

1 tbsp sunflower oil

1cm (½in) piece of ginger, peeled and grated

1 clove of garlic, finely sliced

1 spring onion (scallion), finely sliced

4 florets of long-stem broccoli

Handful of cashew nuts

3 tbsp dark soy sauce

1 tsp toasted sesame oil

½ tsp Chinese five spice

Pinch of caster (superfine) sugar

150g (5½oz) straight-to-wok noodles (ensure egg free)

2 radishes, finely sliced

½ tsp sesame seeds

Heat the sunflower oil in a wok over a high heat until hot. Throw in the ginger, garlic and spring onion, and stir-fry for 1 minute to infuse the oil.

Throw in the broccoli and cashew nuts, and stir-fry for 1 minute.

Pour in the soy sauce, sesame oil, Chinese five spice and sugar, and stir-fry for 2 minutes.

Add the noodles, separating them gently, then stir to coat the noodles in the sauce. Cook for a further 2 minutes until the noodles are piping hot, then remove from the heat.

Scatter with the finely sliced radishes and sesame seeds, and serve immediately.

laksa noodles

Serves 2 generously

The perfect weekend lunch – fast and on a budget! These noodles strike the perfect balance of heat, spice, creaminess and zest. Find coconut milk cheaper in the world food aisle of large supermarkets, or opt for own-brand varieties, which are considerably cheaper than branded versions.

———————

TIP Ready-to-wok noodles are great to keep in your store cupboard for a fast addition to stir-fries or eastern-style curries. Ensure they are egg free, or try soft rice noodles.

1 tbsp sunflower oil

2 red chillies, deseeded and chopped

2cm (¾in) piece of ginger, peeled and grated

3 cloves of garlic, peeled and crushed

1 tsp Chinese five spice

1 tbsp light soy sauce

4 spring onions (scallions), finely chopped

1 carrot, peeled and roughly sliced

6 sugar snap peas, halved diagonally

1 red (bell) pepper, deseeded and finely sliced

400ml (14fl oz) can full-fat coconut milk

1 tbsp smooth peanut butter

300g (10½oz) ready-to-wok soft noodles (ensure egg free)

Juice of ½ unwaxed lime

Handful of coriander (cilantro) leaves, roughly torn

Heat the oil in a large wok over a medium heat, then throw in the chillies, ginger, garlic, Chinese five spice, soy sauce and 3 of the spring onions. Stir-fry for 2 minutes to infuse the oil.

Increase the heat to high and throw in the carrot, sugar snap peas and red pepper, then stir-fry for a further 2 minutes.

Pour in the coconut milk and stir through the peanut butter. Stir to combine and simmer for 5 minutes, stirring frequently.

Carefully add the noodles, stir, and cook for a further 4 minutes.

Remove from the heat and squeeze over the lime juice. Scatter with the coriander leaves and the remaining spring onion. Serve immediately.

orange, pomegranate and pistachio pilaf

Serves 2

With layers of flavour, colour and texture, this three-step rice dish is perfect for sharing and can be served hot or cold, making it ideal for a packed lunch the following day if you have leftovers.

2 tbsp olive oil

1 red onion, finely chopped

250g (9oz/1¼ cups) extra-long-grain basmati rice

600ml (20fl oz/2½ cups) hot vegetable stock

2 tsp harissa paste

1 tsp ground cumin

1 tsp ground turmeric

1 pomegranate

1 unwaxed orange

Handful of shelled pistachios

Generous handful of fresh flat-leaf parsley

Pinch of sea salt

In a large pan, heat the oil over a medium heat. Add the onion to the pan and cook for 2 minutes until softened but not browned.

Add in the rice and coat in the onion oil mixture. Pour in the vegetable stock and increase the heat to medium–high.

Spoon in the harissa, cumin and turmeric and cook for 10 minutes until the stock has absorbed, stirring frequently to prevent sticking.

In the meantime, halve the pomegranate and scoop out the seeds, reserving them in a bowl. Halve the orange and roughly chop the pistachios and parsley.

Remove the pilaf from the heat and stir through the pomegranate seeds, pistachios and parsley. Squeeze over the orange juice and season with sea salt to serve.

apricot, pistachio and mint pilaf

Serves 2

This simple and beautiful pilaf uses bulgur wheat as a base, with a flavour twist on the traditional side salad tabbouleh. Sweet dried apricots, fragrant pistachios and refreshing mint are brought together with lemon juice to create the perfect sharing side dish.

TIP Save time by chopping the herbs, pistachios and apricots while the bulgur wheat is soaking.

100g (3½oz/generous ½ cup) bulgur wheat

Generous handful of fresh mint leaves, finely chopped

Generous handful of fresh flat-leaf parsley, finely chopped

15 soft dried apricots, finely chopped

3 tbsp shelled pistachios, roughly chopped

Generous drizzle of extra virgin olive oil

1 unwaxed lemon, sliced

Generous pinch of sea salt

1 pomegranate

Place the bulgur wheat into a small bowl and pour over enough boiling-hot water to cover. Place a plate over the bowl to form a seal and to aid absorption of the water into the wheat. Leave to stand for 10 minutes.

In the meantime, halve the pomegranate and scoop out the seeds, reserving them in a bowl.

Spoon the bulgur wheat into a mixing bowl and stir in the mint, parsley, apricots and pistachios.

Stir through the pomegranate seeds, extra virgin olive oil and lemon slices, then sprinkle through the sea salt. Mix until combined.

red coconut bisque

Serves 4

This indulgent bisque is silky, creamy and fragrant. It's a seriously addictive bowl of indulgence.

——————

TIP Store-bought Thai red curry paste is a time-saver as the spices are pre-mixed – just ensure it does not contain fish sauce. Keep this handy little jar in the refrigerator for up to four weeks.

2 tsp olive oil

1 onion, finely chopped

2 cloves of garlic, crushed

2cm (¾in) piece of ginger, peeled and finely chopped

1 heaped tbsp Thai red curry paste (ensure vegan)

400ml (14fl oz) can full-fat coconut milk

800ml (28fl oz/3½ cups) hot vegetable stock

2 carrots, grated

6 tomatoes, roughly chopped

Handful of coconut flakes

1 unwaxed lime

Handful of fresh coriander (cilantro), roughly chopped

2 spring onions (scallions), sliced on the diagonal

In a large pan, heat the oil over a low–medium heat. Add the onion to the pan and cook for 2 minutes. Add the garlic and ginger and cook for a further minute, along with the Thai red curry paste.

Pour in the coconut milk and vegetable stock and increase the heat to medium–high. Bring to the boil. Add the carrots and tomatoes to the pan and cook for 8 minutes, stirring occasionally.

Add the coconut flakes to a dry pan and toast over a medium heat for 2 minutes, then set aside.

Remove the bisque pan from the heat and transfer to a blender, or use a hand-held blender and blitz until completely smooth. Squeeze in the lime juice through a sieve and pour into bowls. Scatter with the coriander, spring onions and coconut flakes just before serving.

spinach, chickpea and lemon pilaf

Serves 4

Try this simple one-pot dish for a warming lunch, or serve it cold as a sharing side dish.

———

TIP Frozen spinach also works well in this dish, if you have no fresh spinach available. If using frozen, add it in step 2, to cook with the rice and stock.

1 tbsp sunflower oil

1 red onion, peeled and finely chopped

1 tsp ground turmeric

1 tsp ground cumin

1 tsp garam masala

¼ tsp dried chilli flakes (red pepper flakes)

250g (9oz/1¼ cups) basmati rice

600ml (20fl oz/2½ cups) hot vegetable stock

400g (14oz) can chickpeas, drained and rinsed

4 generous handfuls of spinach leaves

Juice of 1 unwaxed lemon

Generous handful of coriander (cilantro) leaves, finely chopped

Generous pinch of sea salt flakes

Heat the oil in a large saucepan over a medium–high heat and cook the onion for 2 minutes until softened but not browned. Add the turmeric, cumin, garam masala and chilli flakes and stir through for 1 minute.

Pour in the rice and vegetable stock, reduce the heat to medium, then simmer for 8 minutes, stirring frequently to avoid the rice sticking.

Add the chickpeas and spinach leaves and cook for a further 2 minutes.

Remove from the heat and stir through the lemon juice and coriander. Season with sea salt.

herby pea soup

Serves 4

I love this store-cupboard soup, which is creamy and vibrant, as well as being ready to eat in less than 15 minutes.

——————

TIP This soup is delicious for lunch on the go. Ladle into an insulated flask while hot and swirl over the soya cream just before eating.

1 tbsp olive oil

1 onion, finely chopped

1 clove of garlic, crushed

Pinch of dried chilli flakes (red pepper flakes), plus extra for garnish

300g (10½oz/2½ cups) frozen peas

800ml (28fl oz/3½ cups) hot vegetable stock

Generous handful of fresh flat-leaf parsley, finely chopped

Generous handful of fresh mint leaves, finely chopped

Generous pinch of sea salt flakes and freshly ground black pepper

Juice of ½ unwaxed lemon

4 tbsp soya cream, to finish

Heat the olive oil in a large saucepan over a medium heat and cook the onion for 2–3 minutes until softened but not browned. Add the garlic and chilli flakes, and cook for a further minute.

Pour in the frozen peas and vegetable stock and cook for 10 minutes.

Remove from the heat and carefully ladle into a high-powered blender. Blitz until smooth, then stir in the parsley and mint. Season to taste with sea salt and black pepper, then squeeze in the lemon juice.

Pour into bowls and finish with a swirl of soya cream, and a sprinkle of chilli flakes if you like

sweetcorn chowder

Serves 4

I love the smoky background to this classic soup, which is sunny in both colour and flavour. Using frozen sweetcorn reduces the cooking time and it's likely you'll always have some in the freezer ready to make this hearty soup.

———

TIP Smoked paprika deepens the flavour of this chowder and makes it taste as though it has been cooking for hours, not for less than 15 minutes!

1 tbsp sunflower oil

1 onion, roughly chopped

1 red (bell) pepper, finely sliced

1 celery stick, chopped

¼ tsp chilli flakes (red pepper flakes)

300g (10½oz/2 cups) frozen sweetcorn

800ml (28fl oz/3½ cups) hot vegetable stock

400ml (14fl oz) can full-fat coconut milk

1 rounded tsp smoked paprika

Pinch of sea salt

2 spring onions (scallions), sliced on the diagonal

Handful of fresh coriander (cilantro)

1 lime, quartered

In a large pan, heat the oil over a medium heat. Add the onion, then throw the red pepper, celery and chilli flakes into the pan and cook for 2–3 minutes until softened.

Tip in the sweetcorn, vegetable stock and coconut milk and increase the heat to high. Stir through the smoked paprika, then partially cover with a lid. Cook for 10 minutes, stirring occasionally.

Remove from the heat and season with sea salt. Ladle half the soup into a blender and blast until completely smooth. Pour the smooth half back into the unblended soup and combine. Serve hot with spring onions, coriander and a wedge of lime to garnish.

caribbean-style sweet potato and coconut soup

Serves 4

This silken soup tastes as if it has been slow cooked, with a warming spice blend, rich coconut milk and fragrant herbs. The key to cooking this soup in 15 minutes is grating the sweet potato. This exposes more surface area to the heat, therefore creating a faster cooking time. It's all in the science!

─────

TIP Jerk seasoning is a pre-blended spice mix of ground chillies, thyme, allspice, cinnamon and hot cayenne pepper. It's great to keep in the cupboard for easy Jamaican-style curries, or to sprinkle over cooked chips/fries for a fiery flavour twist.

Suitable for freezing.

2 tbsp sunflower oil

2 sweet potatoes, peeled and grated

1 onion, peeled and diced

1 yellow (bell) pepper, deseeded and roughly chopped

2 tsp jerk seasoning

400ml (14fl oz) can full-fat coconut milk

800ml (28fl oz/3½ cups) hot vegetable stock

Generous handful of coriander (cilantro) leaves, some reserved for garnishing

Juice of 1 unwaxed lime

Pinch of sea salt flakes and freshly ground black pepper

Heat the oil in a large saucepan over a medium–high heat and cook the sweet potatoes, onion, yellow pepper and jerk seasoning for 3–4 minutes, stirring constantly, until the onion has begun to soften.

Pour in the coconut milk and vegetable stock, and loosely cover with a lid. Simmer for 10 minutes, then remove from the heat.

Stir in the coriander leaves, then blend until completely smooth using a hand blender or jug blender.

Squeeze in the lime juice and season with sea salt and black pepper. Garnish with the reserved coriander leaves just before serving.

courgette, pea and watercress minestrone

Serves 4

This is a traditional soup with a seasonal twist. Spring pea and courgette offer a fresher flavour to this soup. Although it's a light meal it will satisfy all the family. I use small strands of broken spaghetti in this dish as it's something I always have in my store cupboard, but feel free to experiment with other small pasta varieties. Keep this soup chunky and serve it with wedges of crusty bread.

TIP Suitable for freezing.

1 tbsp sunflower oil

1 onion, roughly chopped

100g (3½oz) asparagus tips

1 medium courgette (zucchini), chopped

2 celery sticks, chopped

300ml (10½fl oz/1¼ cups) hot vegetable stock

400g (14oz) can chopped tomatoes

2 tsp dried mixed herbs

30g (1oz) dried spaghetti

2 handfuls of watercress

3 tbsp frozen peas

Handful of fresh flat-leaf parsley, roughly chopped

Pinch of sea salt flakes and freshly ground black pepper

Heat the oil in a large pan over a medium heat, then add the onion and asparagus tips. Allow to cook for 2 minutes, then add the courgette and celery to the pan along with the vegetable stock.

Tip in the tomatoes and mixed herbs, and increase the heat to high. Break the spaghetti into small pieces and add to the pan. Cover with a lid and cook for 10 minutes, stirring occasionally.

Stir through the watercress and peas, cooking for a further minute. Scatter over the parsley as you remove the pan from the heat. Season with sea salt and black pepper.

rustic ribollita

Serves 2

Traditional Italian ribollita is a hearty and economical dish that uses up kitchen leftovers, including bread. It's somewhere between a stew and a soup, with a chunky yet starchy base and a substantial bite from the cannellini beans. If you've got time to make this the night before you eat it, the flavours will deepen; if you eat it straight away, the dish will be a touch milder, yet still delicious.

TIP Reserve a few pieces of torn bread and fry in 1 tablespoon of olive oil until golden and crisp. Add to the bowls just before serving.

3 slices of white bread

800ml (28fl oz/3½ cups) good-quality hot vegetable stock

1 tbsp olive oil

1 onion, roughly chopped

1 carrot, finely sliced

1 celery stick, sliced

3 cloves of garlic, crushed

4 leaves of cavolo nero

400g (14oz) can chopped tomatoes

235g (8oz) can cannellini beans, drained and rinsed

Pinch of dried rosemary

Pinch of chilli flakes (red pepper flakes)

Pinch of sea salt

Tear the bread into small pieces and place into the jug of vegetable stock to soften.

In a large pan, heat the oil over a medium–high heat. Add the onion, carrot and celery to the pan and cook for 2–3 minutes until the carrot begins to soften.

Add the garlic to the pan. Tear the leafy parts of the cavolo nero and throw them into the pan, discarding the tough stems. Stir-fry for 1 minute.

Tip in the tomatoes and cannellini beans. Pour in the stock and softened bread, along with the rosemary and chilli flakes, bringing to the boil over a high heat. Cook for 10 minutes, stirring frequently.

Remove from the heat and season with sea salt to serve.

gigantes plaki

Serves 2 as a main, or more as part of a mezze

These Greek-style beans are usually slow baked, but I love this quick recipe that will have them on the table within 15 minutes. Serve hot with crusty bread or sliced potatoes, or allow them to cool and enjoy as part of a mezze with Spiced flatbreads (page 63).

TIP Don't skimp on fresh herbs for this recipe! The freshness is what makes gigantes plaki unique. Save time by chopping the herbs while the other ingredients are cooking.

Suitable for freezing.

1 tbsp sunflower oil

1 onion, peeled and finely chopped

1 stick of celery, finely diced

1 carrot, peeled and finely chopped

1 clove of garlic, peeled and crushed

1 tsp sweet paprika

1 tsp dried oregano

½ tsp mild chilli powder

½ tsp ground cinnamon

400g (14oz) can chopped tomatoes

1 tsp granulated sugar

400g (14oz) can butter (lima) beans, drained and rinsed

2 tbsp tomato ketchup

Generous handful of flat-leaf parsley, finely chopped

Small handful of mint leaves, finely chopped

Generous pinch of sea salt flakes

Heat the oil in a large saucepan over a medium–high heat and cook the onion, celery and carrot for 2–3 minutes until beginning to soften.

Add the garlic, paprika, oregano, chilli powder and cinnamon and cook for a further minute.

Pour in the tomatoes, sugar, butter beans and ketchup, then reduce the heat to medium. Cook for 10 minutes, stirring frequently.

Remove the pan from the heat, then stir through the parsley and mint. Season with sea salt.

aubergine caponata

Serves 2 generously

This simple recipe from Sicily combines both fresh and store-cupboard ingredients to create a delicious lunch or starter. Traditionally, it is served at room temperature, but it also tastes excellent when hot. Serve this sweet-and-sour dish with warm ciabatta.

———

TIP For a more substantial dish, or to stretch it to serve more people, add a can of drained and rinsed cannellini beans

2 tbsp sunflower oil

1 aubergine (eggplant), chopped into 3cm (1¼in) cubes

1 tsp dried oregano

1 red onion, peeled and finely sliced

1 clove of garlic, peeled and finely sliced

8 cherry tomatoes

1 tbsp sultanas (golden raisins)

1 tbsp balsamic vinegar

10 green olives, pitted and halved

Juice of ¼ unwaxed lemon

Generous handful of basil leaves

Pinch of sea salt flakes

Heat the oil in a large frying pan over a high heat and cook the aubergine and oregano for 5 minutes until starting to soften.

Reduce the heat to medium–high, then add the onion and garlic and cook for 2 minutes.

Add the cherry tomatoes, sultanas and balsamic vinegar, stir through and cook to reduce for 5 minutes, then stir through the olives.

Remove from the heat and squeeze in the lemon juice. Scatter with the basil leaves and sea salt flakes just before serving.

savoury pancakes with garlicky mushrooms

Serves 2 generously (makes about 6)

A simple, thrifty, yet luxurious dinner that transforms basic ingredients into a hearty meal. Why wait until Shrove Tuesday to flip the pancake pan? Soya cream is cost effective and available in most supermarkets. The UHT varieties tend to be cheaper, and last for longer before use.

TIP A hand-held balloon whisk is a cheap, essential tool for your utensil drawer, and it mixes the smoothest pancake batter.

For the pancakes

100g (3½oz/¾ cup) plain (all-purpose) flour

200ml (7fl oz/scant 1 cup) unsweetened soya milk, chilled

Generous pinch of fine sea salt

6 tbsp sunflower oil

For the garlicky mushrooms

1 tbsp sunflower oil

200g (7oz) button mushrooms, some sliced, some whole

3 cloves of garlic, peeled and finely sliced

6 tbsp soya cream

Small handful of flat-leaf parsley, finely chopped

Generous pinch of sea salt and freshly ground black pepper

Start by making the pancakes. Whisk together the flour, soya milk, and sea salt in a bowl until smooth.

Heat 1 tablespoon of the oil in a frying pan over a medium heat. Test if the oil is hot by adding a drop of pancake batter to the pan: if it sizzles and becomes golden within 30 seconds, it is at optimum temperature. Add 4 tablespoons of the batter to make one pancake and swirl the batter around the pan to coat the base evenly.

When the pancake is golden after 2–3 minutes, carefully flip it over to cook the other side. Drain on paper towels, then keep warm in the oven while you continue to cook the other pancakes, using a tablespoon of the oil for each.

For the garlicky mushrooms, heat the oil in a separate frying pan over a medium–high heat and cook the mushrooms for 5 minutes, stirring frequently.

Add the garlic and cook for a further minute. Remove from the heat and stir in the soya cream and parsley. Season with sea salt and black pepper.

To assemble, place the pancakes on serving plates and generously load on the garlicky mushrooms. Fold the pancakes over and serve while hot.

charred courgette and pesto tart

Serves 4

Create this simple yet delicious tart by baking the puff pastry in the oven while you grill the courgettes. This reduces the cooking time and prevents the dreaded 'soggy bottom'. Charred courgettes pair well with the flavour of fresh pesto, but experiment with other quick-cook green vegetables, including asparagus, broad (fava) beans, spinach and peas.

TIP Use up any remaining pesto as a pasta sauce.

1 sheet of puff pastry (ensure dairy free)

2 tsp unsweetened soya milk

1 tbsp sunflower oil

2 medium courgettes (zucchini), sliced into rounds and ribbons

1 clove of garlic, peeled

Generous handful of basil leaves (reserve a few leaves for garnish)

1 tbsp flaked (slivered) almonds

Juice of ¼ unwaxed lemon

Generous drizzle of extra virgin olive oil

Generous pinch of sea salt flakes and freshly ground black pepper

Preheat the oven to 220°C/425°F/Gas 7.

Place the puff pastry on a baking tray and fold over each of the four sides to create a 1cm (½in) crust, then brush the crust with the soya milk. Use a fork to lightly prick the centre of the pastry. Bake for 10–12 minutes until the edges have risen and become golden.

While the pastry base is cooking, prepare the filling. Brush a griddle pan with the sunflower oil and place over a medium–high heat. Use tongs to lay the courgette rounds and ribbons onto the hot pan and cook for 5 minutes, then carefully turn and cook for a further 3 minutes.

To make the pesto, add the garlic, basil and flaked almonds to a food processor or blender and blitz until semi-smooth. Pour in the lemon juice and extra virgin olive oil and blitz again to combine. Season with sea salt flakes. Alternatively, make the pesto by very finely chopping the garlic, basil and flaked almonds before stirring in the lemon juice, extra virgin olive oil and seasoning.

Remove the pastry from the oven, then generously spread the inner section with some pesto. Arrange the courgettes neatly over the pesto, then brush the courgettes with a little more pesto. Scatter with a few basil leaves and season with black pepper.

sweet potatoes with yogurt, pomegranate and toasted walnuts

Serves 2

Everyone loves an oven-baked jacket potato. That savoury-sweet taste is a true home comfort; however, there are times when you need that comfort fast. I love making sweet jacket potatoes in the microwave; brushing the skin with a little olive oil helps to crisp them up, and their lingering sweetness is reminiscent of that of an oven-baked spud. Load with your favourite toppings, or with mine, which are yogurt, pomegranate and walnuts.

2 large sweet potatoes

2 tsp olive oil

2 tbsp walnuts

1 pomegranate

4 tbsp unsweetened soya yogurt

Generous handful of fresh flat-leaf parsley, finely chopped

Pinch of sea salt

Thoroughly wash and dry the sweet potatoes. Brush the skins with the oil, then cook together in an 850W microwave for 8–9 minutes, until a knife can pierce through the filling effortlessly.

While the sweet potatoes are cooking, add the walnuts to a dry pan and toast over a high heat for 2–3 minutes, then set aside.

Slice the pomegranate and gently remove the seeds.

Remove the cooked sweet potatoes from the microwave and carefully slice them down the centre. Generously spoon in the yogurt and scatter over the toasted walnuts, pomegranate seeds and parsley. Season with sea salt.

TIP Stir through 1 teaspoon of harissa to the yogurt for added heat, if you like.

moroccan-style flatbread pizza

Serves 1

Go home, kick off your shoes and make this pizza. It's everything a pizza should be – and then some.

TIP Harissa is a spicy paste mix, made from chillies, tomatoes and rose water. You will find it in most supermarkets, or Middle Eastern shops and delis.

1 tbsp olive oil

1 large onion, finely sliced

1 tbsp tomato purée

2 tsp harissa

1 large flatbread

Generous handful of baby spinach leaves

Generous drizzle of extra virgin olive oil

1 rounded tbsp pine nuts

1 tbsp pomegranate seeds

Small handful of fresh flat-leaf parsley, roughly torn

Juice of ¼ unwaxed lemon

Preheat the oven to 200°C/400°F/Gas 6.

Meanwhile, heat the olive oil in a frying pan over a medium–high heat and cook the onion for 8 minutes until golden and softened.

Mix together the tomato purée and harissa. Arrange the flatbread on a baking tray, then spread over the spicy tomato mixture.

Scatter over the spinach leaves, then drizzle with extra virgin olive oil. Spoon over the golden onions and scatter with the pine nuts.

Bake for 5–6 minutes until hot, then scatter with the pomegranate seeds and parsley. Drizzle over the lemon juice just before serving.

chilli bean sliders

Serves 4

Treat yourself to these spicy, mini burgers. Little hands will love mashing and stirring the slider mix! Load with Sweetcorn salsa (page 290) and pickled gherkins.

TIP Keep the cans of kidney beans refrigerated before use, for a firmer mixture that is less likely to break in the pan.

Suitable for freezing.

2 x 400g (14oz) cans chilled kidney beans, drained and rinsed

1 yellow (bell) pepper, deseeded and finely diced

2 spring onions (scallions), finely chopped

Handful of coriander (cilantro) leaves, torn

4 tbsp rolled oats

1 tsp mild chilli powder

1 tsp smoked paprika

½ tsp fine sea salt

6 tbsp sunflower oil, for frying

8 mini white bread buns (ensure vegan)

4 pickled gherkins, sliced

Sweetcorn salsa (page 290), to serve

In a large bowl, mash the chilled kidney beans using a fork (or squeeze in your hands) until just a few beans remain whole. The mixture should be semi-smooth.

Add the yellow pepper, spring onions, coriander, oats, chilli powder, smoked paprika and sea salt, then stir until everything is combined into a dense mixture.

Heat the oil in a large frying pan over a medium heat. Make eight ball shapes from the bean mixture, then flatten into patties. Carefully place in the hot pan and cook for 4 minutes on each side, flipping with a spatula.

Serve the sliders in toasted or warmed mini bread buns, with sliced gherkins and a spoonful of sweetcorn salsa.

BIGGER
THINGS

tuscan bean and pasta soup

Serves 4

The reassuring texture and flavour of white beans and pasta are brought together in this simple soup, which is filling and warming.

──────────

TIP Any small or spoon-sized pastas work well in this soup, including orzo or margheritine.

1 tbsp olive oil

1 onion, finely chopped

1 stick of celery, finely chopped

1 carrot, finely chopped

1 clove of garlic, crushed

1 tsp dried oregano

400g (14oz) can chopped tomatoes

1 litre (1¾ pints/4½ cups) hot vegetable stock

100g (3½oz) farfalle pasta (ensure egg free)

400g (14oz) can cannellini beans, drained and rinsed

Generous handful of kale, stalks removed

Sea salt and freshly ground black pepper

Heat the olive oil in a large saucepan over a medium–high heat and cook the onion, celery and carrot for 3–4 minutes, stirring frequently. Add the garlic and oregano, and cook for a further minute.

Pour in the chopped tomatoes, hot vegetable stock, pasta and cannellini beans, and cook for 8 minutes, with the pan lid placed over on an angle. Stir occasionally.

Add the kale and cook for a further 2 minutes.

Season to taste with sea salt and black pepper.

yasai miso ramen

Serves 2

This is the ultimate meal in a bowl. 'Yasai' is the Japanese word for vegetable. In this dish, vegetables are simmered with ramen noodles in a fragrant stock, seasoned with white miso. Pile your bowl up high!

———

TIP You can find miso in many supermarkets and health-food shops – I find that white miso has a milder flavour than red or mixed pastes.

1 tbsp sunflower oil

2 cloves of garlic, grated

2cm (¾in) piece of ginger, peeled and grated

2 red chillies: 1 finely chopped, 1 deseeded and finely sliced

600ml (20fl oz/2½ cups) hot water

1 rounded tsp white miso paste

½ tsp Chinese five spice

2 whole star anise

1 carrot, finely sliced

1 red (bell) pepper, finely sliced

6 leaves of pak choi (bok choy), finely sliced

6 florets of long-stem broccoli

150g (5½oz) dried ramen noodles (egg free)

2 spring onions (scallions), finely chopped

Handful of fresh coriander (cilantro), finely chopped

Juice of 1 unwaxed lime

1 tbsp white sesame seeds

Heat the oil in a large pan over a medium–high heat. Add the garlic and ginger to the pan, along with the chopped chilli.

Pour in the hot water and stir through the white miso paste. Sprinkle in the Chinese five spice and star anise and bring to the boil for 5 minutes.

While the stock is boiling, remove the star anise. Add the carrot, red pepper, pak choi and broccoli to the pan. Add the dried ramen noodles and cook for 5–6 minutes until the vegetables are bright and the noodles have softened.

Remove the pan from the heat and ladle into bowls. Scatter with the spring onions and coriander, and squeeze over the lime juice. Sprinkle with the sesame seeds and sliced red chilli to serve.

five-minute rainbow noodles

Serves 2 generously

Cook up a rainbow in the kitchen with these 5-minute noodles. If you have time earlier in the day, finely chop the vegetables and keep them chilled before cooking them up for dinner.

TIP Younger eaters will love these speedy and colourful noodles; simply omit the red chilli to reduce the heat.

2 tbsp sunflower oil

¼ red cabbage, finely sliced

1 carrot, peeled and very finely sliced

1 yellow (bell) pepper, deseeded and very finely sliced

2 spring onions (scallions), roughly chopped

1 red chilli, deseeded and sliced

300g (10½oz) ready-to-wok soft noodles (ensure egg free)

2 tbsp sweet chilli sauce (ensure vegan)

Juice of ½ unwaxed lime

1 tbsp salted peanuts, roughly chopped

Handful of coriander (cilantro) leaves, roughly torn

Heat the oil in a wok over a high heat, then stir-fry the cabbage, carrot, yellow pepper, spring onions and chilli for 2 minutes.

Add the noodles, then stir through the sweet chilli sauce and stir-fry everything for a further 2 minutes.

Squeeze in the lime juice and sprinkle with the peanuts. Scatter with the coriander leaves just before serving.

korean-style bibimbap bowls

Serves 2

Eat through the mountain of hot, sweet vegetables to a base of crisp, fried rice. Cooked, leftover basmati rice works best in this recipe, as it is fragrant and naturally starchy.

TIP There's no need to buy pricey pre-cooked rice; simply simmer basmati rice for 12 minutes, drain, then allow to cool completely before using in this recipe.

3 tbsp sunflower oil

6 tbsp cooked or leftover basmati rice

10 button mushrooms, brushed clean

4 radishes, finely sliced

1 carrot, peeled and very finely sliced

1 small courgette (zucchini), very finely sliced

2 tbsp frozen or fresh podded edamame (soya) beans

Handful of spinach leaves

1 tbsp dark soy sauce

½ tsp soft brown sugar

1 red chilli, deseeded and finely sliced

1 spring onion (scallion), finely sliced

1 tbsp sesame seeds

Heat 2 tablespoons of the oil in a medium-sized frying pan over a medium–high heat, then add the cooked rice, pushing it down flat to form a level rice cake. Cook for 5 minutes until the base of the rice becomes crisp, then remove and separate into two bowls.

Heat the remaining tablespoon of oil in a large wok over a high heat and stir-fry the mushrooms, radishes, carrot, courgette, edamame beans and spinach leaves for 2–3 minutes. Spoon in the soy sauce and brown sugar, then stir-fry for a further 2 minutes.

Spoon the vegetables over the rice, then scatter with the fresh chilli, spring onion and sesame seeds.

sweet-stuffed ramiro peppers with salted lemon yogurt

Serves 2

Try to source Ramiro peppers as they have a thinner skin than regular bell peppers, so they roast faster with a sweet, smoky taste.

──────────

TIP If you don't have Ramiro peppers available, standard bell peppers will cook in around 20 minutes.

1 tbsp olive oil

1 onion, finely sliced

6 Ramiro peppers

200g (7oz/1¼ cups) couscous

200ml (7fl oz/scant 1 cup) hot vegetable stock

Small handful of fresh flat-leaf parsley, finely chopped

Small handful of fresh coriander (cilantro), finely chopped

¼ tsp ground cinnamon

¼ tsp ground mixed spice (pumpkin pie spice)

1 tbsp plump sultanas (golden raisins)

1 tbsp flaked (slivered) almonds

For the yogurt dressing

4 tbsp unsweetened soya yogurt

Pinch of sea salt

Juice of ½ unwaxed lemon

Preheat the oven to 200°C/400°F/Gas 6.

Heat the oil in a pan over a low heat. Add the onion and fry for 10 minutes until browned.

Slice the peppers in half lengthways, removing the seeds and inner stem. Place on a baking tray and roast for 10 minutes.

In the meantime, tip the couscous into a small bowl with the hot vegetable stock. Cover with a lid and allow the stock to absorb for five minutes. When the couscous is light and fluffy, fork through and stir in the finely chopped parsley and coriander.

Add the cooked onion to the couscous. Sprinkle in the cinnamon and mixed spice and stir through the sultanas and flaked almonds. Spoon the onion and couscous filling into the peppers and keep warm.

To make the dressing, whisk the yogurt and salt in a bowl with the lemon juice. Spoon over the stuffed peppers just before serving.

Serve with Caramelized red onion houmous (page 279).

harissa aubergine kebabs with cucumber, red onion and mint relish

Serves 2 generously

These spicy, sweet, and satisfyingly sticky kebabs are made for summer. Simply grill or barbecue! Serve in soft flatbreads with the tangy relish and jewel-like pomegranate seeds and a generous drizzle of tahini.

———

TIP Once exclusive to Middle-Eastern grocery shops, harissa is now available in most large supermarkets – simply check out the world-food aisle.

1 large aubergine (eggplant), cut into 3cm (1¼in) chunks

6 whole cherry tomatoes

2 tbsp harissa paste

1 tbsp maple syrup

2 large flatbreads

1 small pomegranate, seeds only

Generous drizzle of tahini paste

For the relish
¼ small cucumber, finely chopped

1 small red onion, finely chopped

Handful of fresh mint leaves, roughly chopped

1 tbsp cider vinegar

Heat a griddle pan over a medium–high heat. Thread the aubergine chunks and cherry tomatoes onto two metal or pre-soaked wooden skewers.

Whisk the harissa paste and maple syrup in a large bowl, then dip the skewers into the mixture, generously coating the aubergine and tomatoes. Place the skewers onto the griddle pan for 5–6 minutes, then turn on the other side and cook for a further 5 minutes.

In the meantime, prepare the relish. Put the cucumber and red onion in a small bowl and stir through the mint. Sprinkle over the vinegar and allow to infuse while the kebabs are cooking.

Arrange the grilled flatbreads on a platter and liberally sprinkle over the pomegranate seeds. Carefully remove the kebabs from the griddle pan and slide off the vegetables onto the flatbreads. Spoon over the relish and tahini and serve immediately.

lentil, rice and caramelized onion salad

Serves 4

Simple, delicious, budget-friendly comfort food that will become a classic in your kitchen.

———

TIP This dish is also delicious served chilled as a sharing pilaf.

180g (6oz/1 cup) basmati rice

2 tbsp sunflower oil

3 large red onions, peeled and finely sliced

2 tsp soft brown sugar

½ tsp ground cumin

½ tsp ground cinnamon

½ tsp ground turmeric

½ tsp mild chilli powder

400g (14oz) can green lentils, drained and rinsed

Small handful of flat-leaf parsley, roughly chopped

2 tbsp unsweetened soya yogurt

Juice of ¼ unwaxed lemon

Generous pinch of sea salt flakes

In a large saucepan, add the basmati rice and cover with cold water. Bring to the boil over a medium–high heat for 12 minutes, stirring occasionally, until the water is absorbed and the rice appears fluffy, then set aside.

In the meantime, heat the oil in a large frying pan over a high heat and cook the onions for 5 minutes, then add the brown sugar and cook for a further 5 minutes until caramelized, stirring frequently.

Add the cumin, cinnamon, turmeric and chilli powder to the onions, then cook for a further minute.

Tip the spiced onions and any remaining oil into the rice, along with the lentils. Return to the heat and stir through for 1 minute.

Scatter over the parsley and divide into warmed bowls. Spoon on the soya yogurt, squeeze over the lemon juice and season with sea salt.

double-decker
spicy falafel burger

Serves 1

There are times when you need more than a bite-size falafel in a flatbread. Those times call for thick, spicy burgers layered with onion and houmous in a toasted, seeded bun. There's no need for manners here, just get stuck in!

TIP If you have time, allow the burger mix to chill in the refrigerator for 30 minutes. This will help the ingredients to firm up and avoid cracking in the hot pan.

For the burgers
400g (14oz) can chickpeas, drained and rinsed

2 rounded tsp ground cumin

½ tsp smoked paprika

½ tsp dried chilli flakes (red pepper flakes)

2 handfuls of fresh coriander (cilantro) with stalks

1 handful of fresh flat-leaf parsley with stalks

1 tsp harissa paste

1 slice of white bread, grated into breadcrumbs

1 tbsp sesame seeds

4 tbsp sunflower oil

For the additions
1 large seeded white bread bun, halved

½ baby gem lettuce, tough stems discarded and roughly sliced

1 tbsp houmous

½ red onion, sliced into 4 rings

1 tbsp chutney of choice

To make the burgers, add the chickpeas, cumin, smoked paprika, chilli flakes, coriander, parsley and harissa to a high-powered blender or food processor and blitz until semi-smooth. Leave some chunks to add some bite.

Carefully remove the mixture from the blender or food processor and shape into two flat burgers.

Mix the breadcrumbs and sesame seeds in a small, shallow dish and gently press the burgers into them.

Heat the oil in a frying pan over a medium–high heat until hot. Carefully add the burgers to the pan and cook for 4–5 minutes on each side until golden.

In the meantime, heat a dry griddle pan over a high heat and toast the bread bun for 2 minutes. Remove from the heat and layer the lettuce onto one half of the bun.

Place the first burger onto the lettuce and add the chutney, then add the second burger and spoon on the houmous and onion rings. Top with the other bun half. Serve immediately.

grilled pepper fajitas

Serves 2

Revive those wrinkly peppers with this family-friendly recipe. Fajita spice mixes can be expensive, so make your own using spices that are already in your cupboard – make a big batch so you always have some to hand.

TIP Soft tortilla wraps freeze well and defrost within a few minutes, so store them in the freezer and take out the amount you need to avoid waste.

2 tbsp sunflower oil

1 red (bell) pepper, deseeded and cut into 3cm (1¼in) slices

1 yellow (bell) pepper, deseeded and cut into 3cm (1¼in) slices

2 red onions, peeled and finely sliced

400g (14oz) can red kidney beans, drained and rinsed

For the seasoning mix
1 tbsp mild chilli powder

1 tsp smoked paprika

½ tsp garlic powder

½ tsp ground cumin

½ tsp fine sea salt

To serve
2–4 soft tortilla wraps, warmed

1 baby gem lettuce, roughly cut into wedges

2 tbsp vegan cream cheese

Small handful of coriander (cilantro), torn

Juice of ½ unwaxed lime

Brush a griddle pan with 1 tablespoon of the oil and heat over a medium–high heat.

Use tongs to carefully place the pepper slices onto the hot griddle pan. Allow to sizzle for 5 minutes, turn to the other side, and griddle for a further 3 minutes until grill marks appear.

Heat the remaining tablespoon of oil in a wok or large frying pan over a medium–high heat and add the red onions and red kidney beans, along with the chilli powder, smoked paprika, garlic powder, ground cumin and sea salt, then stir-fry for 5 minutes until fragrant and the beans are coated in the spices. Remove from the heat.

Carefully transfer the grilled peppers from the griddle pan into the wok. Stir to combine.

Fill the warmed tortilla wraps with the cooked vegetables and beans, then add the lettuce, cream cheese and coriander. Squeeze over the lime juice and fold the wraps.

tortilla tacos with refried beans, carrot, chilli and coriander

Serves 4 (Makes 12)

Crispy, golden tacos are filled with smooth refried beans, then topped with a bright carrot salsa. You'll never look at store-bought tacos again! Serve with the Four-ingredient soured cream with chives (page 286).

TIP Pinto beans are traditionally used to make refried beans, and the canned variety mash down really well. If you don't have pinto beans available, red kidney beans make a good alternative, but will need a little more elbow grease when mashing.

For the tortilla tacos

3 tortilla wraps, cut into quarters

1 tsp sunflower oil

For the refried beans

1 tbsp sunflower oil

1 red (bell) pepper, deseeded and roughly chopped

3 spring onions (scallions), finely chopped

1 tsp mild chilli powder

1 tsp smoked paprika

1 tsp garlic powder

2 x 400g (14oz) cans pinto beans, drained and rinsed

Juice of ½ unwaxed lime

For the carrot salad

1 large carrot, peeled and grated

Generous handful of coriander (cilantro) leaves, roughly torn

1 small red chilli, deseeded and finely sliced

Generous pinch of smoked sea salt

Preheat the oven to 200°C/400°F/Gas 6.

Using two deep muffin trays, push a tortilla quarter into each mould to form a cup shape. Brush the edges with the oil, then bake for 8–10 minutes until crisp and light golden.

In the meantime, prepare the refried beans. Heat the oil in a saucepan over a medium heat and cook the red pepper and spring onions for 3 minutes until the pepper begins to soften. Spoon in the chilli powder, smoked paprika and garlic powder and cook for a further minute. Tip in the pinto beans and stir to combine with all the spices. After 3 minutes, remove the pan from the heat, then mash the beans using a potato masher or fork until semi-smooth. Stir in the lime juice.

In a bowl, toss together the carrot, coriander, fresh chilli and smoked sea salt.

To assemble, remove the baked tortilla taco cups from the muffin pan and spoon in the hot refried beans, then load with the carrot salad.

monday's root vegetable bhuna

Serves 2 generously

I always roast up too many vegetables to go with Sunday lunch. Sometimes accidentally, sometimes intentionally; either way, they make a perfect addition to this simple and spicy bhuna.

———

TIP For the perfect roasted root vegetables, drizzle sunflower oil over peeled carrots, parsnips, quartered red onions and squash, then roast at 200°C/ 400°F/Gas 6 for 35–40 minutes, turning once. Allow the leftovers to cool fully, then refrigerate for use the following day.

Suitable for freezing.

1 tbsp sunflower oil

1 onion, peeled and finely chopped

1 red (bell) pepper, finely sliced

2 cloves of garlic, peeled and crushed

1 tsp ground cumin

1 tsp ground turmeric

½ tsp dried chilli flakes (red pepper flakes)

1 tbsp medium curry paste (ensure dairy free)

400g (14oz) can chopped tomatoes

2 handfuls of fresh or frozen spinach

½ roasting tray of leftover roasted root vegetables, including carrots, parsnips, red onion and butternut squash, roughly chopped

Juice of ½ unwaxed lemon

Pinch of sea salt flakes

Heat the oil in a saucepan over a medium–high heat and cook the onion and red pepper for 2 minutes until softened.

Add the garlic, ground cumin, turmeric and chilli flakes and cook for a further 1 minute.

Stir in the curry paste and chopped tomatoes, then reduce the heat to medium. Simmer for 8–9 minutes, then stir in the spinach and cook for a further 2 minutes.

Stir in the leftover roasted root vegetables and squeeze over the lemon juice. Season with sea salt and serve.

garden biryani

Serves 4

Traditionally, biryani is slow-cooked; however, this version lends itself well to fast cooking due to the variety of rice used and the quick-cook vegetables. Adapt the vegetables to what you have available seasonally for an ever-changing dish.

TIP White basmati rice cooks faster than any brown varieties.

1 tbsp sunflower oil

1 onion, finely chopped

½ small cauliflower, broken into florets

12 green beans, ends trimmed

1 yellow (bell) pepper, finely sliced

2 tbsp medium curry paste

1 tsp turmeric

1 tsp ground cumin

½ tsp dried chilli flakes (red pepper flakes)

400g (14oz/2¼ cups) basmati rice

1 litre (1¾ pints/4½ cups) hot vegetable stock

2 tbsp frozen peas

2 tbsp roasted cashew nuts

Juice of 1 unwaxed lemon

Generous handful of fresh coriander (cilantro), roughly torn

1 red chilli, deseeded and finely sliced

Generous pinch of sea salt

Heat the sunflower oil in a large saucepan over a medium–high heat and cook the onion for 1 minute until it begins to soften. Add the cauliflower, green beans and yellow pepper, and sauté for 2–3 minutes.

Spoon in the curry paste, turmeric, cumin and chilli flakes, and stir to coat the vegetables.

Pour in the basmati rice and vegetable stock, then simmer over a medium heat for 9 minutes, stirring frequently.

Stir through the peas and cashew nuts, and cook for a further minute.

Remove from the heat and drizzle over the lemon juice. Scatter with the coriander, fresh red chilli and sea salt just before serving.

pad thai jay with lime and sesame

Serves 2

This is my go-to recipe for when I'm hungry and in a hurry, as it is fast, simple and totally satisfying. I prefer to use low-preparation, fast-cook vegetables; however, feel free to adapt to what you have at home.

TIP Soft noodles reduce the cooking time of this pad Thai jay; however, do ensure they are vegan as some types may contain egg. You're more likely to find the egg-free versions stored on the shelves rather than in the chiller cabinets.

1 tbsp sunflower oil

6 florets of long-stem broccoli

Generous handful of kale

2 small red chillies: 1 finely chopped, 1 deseeded and finely sliced

10 sugar snap peas

8 tbsp light soy sauce

2 packs of soft cooked noodles (egg free)

1 spring onion (scallion), finely sliced

Handful of fresh coriander (cilantro), finely chopped

1 tbsp peanuts, roughly crushed

1 tbsp white sesame seeds

1 unwaxed lime

Heat the oil in a wok over a high heat until smoking hot.

In the meantime, trim any tough stems from the broccoli and kale.

Add the chopped chilli and the broccoli, kale and sugar snap peas to the wok and stir-fry for 3–4 minutes.

Spoon in the soy sauce and stir through. Then add the noodles and continue to stir-fry for 2–3 minutes, being careful not to break the noodles. Cook until all the ingredients are coated in soy sauce, and the vegetables are crisp and bright.

Remove the wok from the heat and stir the spring onion and coriander through the pad Thai jay. Scatter the peanuts over the top along with the sesame seeds and finely sliced red chilli.

Slice the lime in half and squeeze the juice through a sieve onto the noodles. Serve immediately.

soy-glazed butternut green curry

Serves 4

Creamy, delicately spiced Thai-style curry is a crowd-pleaser, and is best shared. Never think less of store-bought curry pastes, they are simply a concentrated spice mix. Check that the curry paste is vegan, as some contain fish sauce.

TIP To make chopping a butternut squash easier, simply blast it in the microwave for a couple of minutes to soften.

For the soy-glazed butternut squash

2 tbsp sunflower oil

1 medium butternut squash, peeled and cut into bite-size cubes

3 tbsp light soy sauce

For the green curry base

1 tbsp sunflower oil

1 stalk of lemongrass, bruised

2 tbsp Thai green curry paste (ensure vegan)

2 x 400ml (14fl oz) cans full-fat coconut milk

Handful of sugar snap peas, halved

Handful of asparagus spears, tough ends removed

Handful of green beans, ends trimmed

2 tbsp frozen or fresh edamame (soya) beans

Juice of 1 unwaxed lime, plus fresh wedges for serving

Generous handful of coriander (cilantro), roughly torn

1 red chilli, deseeded and finely sliced

1 spring onion (scallion), finely chopped

Heat the sunflower oil in a wok while you coat the butternut squash cubes in the soy sauce. Add the soy-coated butternut squash to the wok and cook over a medium–high heat for 10 minutes until softened and browned, stirring frequently.

Move on to the curry base. Heat the sunflower oil in a separate large frying pan. Add the lemongrass and Thai green curry paste, and infuse over a high heat for 1 minute. Stir in the coconut milk, then reduce the heat slightly and simmer for 8 minutes. Remove and discard the lemongrass stalk.

Throw the sugar snap peas, asparagus spears, green beans and edamame beans into the curry sauce and cook for 4–5 minutes until the vegetables are al dente.

Ladle the curry into bowls and spoon in the softened soy-glazed butternut squash. Top each bowl with a squeeze of lime juice and sprinkle with the coriander, a few slices of chilli and a scattering of the chopped spring onion.

roasted broccoli curry

Serves 2 generously

Broccoli takes on a wonderful, nutty flavour when roasted to pack this simple dinner full of flavour. Frozen edamame beans are available in supermarkets or Chinese shops and last for ages in your freezer at home – simply take out the amount you need and cook from frozen.

———————

TIP Suitable for freezing.

For the soy-roasted broccoli
220g (8oz) long-stem broccoli

1 tbsp sunflower oil

2 tbsp light soy sauce

1 tbsp sesame seeds

For the curry
1 tbsp sunflower oil

2 cloves of garlic, peeled and crushed

4 spring onions (scallions), roughly chopped

2 tbsp frozen or fresh podded edamame (soya) beans

1 tbsp Thai green curry paste (ensure vegan)

400ml (14fl oz) can full-fat coconut milk

Generous handful of coriander (cilantro) leaves, roughly torn

1 red chilli, deseeded and finely chopped, plus extra, sliced, to serve

Juice of 1 unwaxed lime, to serve (optional)

Preheat the oven to 200°C/400°F/Gas 6.

Start by roasting the broccoli. Arrange the broccoli on a baking tray and drizzle with the oil. Use a pastry brush to liberally apply the soy sauce over the broccoli, then scatter with the sesame seeds. Roast for 12 minutes until the broccoli has softened and the sesame seeds appear toasted.

In the meantime, prepare the green curry. Heat the oil in a large saucepan over a medium heat and cook the garlic, spring onions and edamame beans for 2 minutes. Stir through the Thai green curry paste and pour in the coconut milk. Simmer for 10 minutes, stirring occasionally.

Remove the pan from the heat and stir through the coriander and chilli.

Ladle the green curry into bowls, then remove the roasted broccoli from the oven and place over the curry. Serve hot with a squeeze of lime, if you like.

rainbow chard, red bean and peanut stew

Serves 4

This is soul food in a bowl. It's creamy and rich with a subtle heat. Rainbow chard adds a pretty array of colours to the stew, but if you don't have any available, you can substitute it for Swiss chard or spring greens. Don't leave out the coriander topping at the end, as this lifts the stew with its fresh flavour. This is one of my favourite foods to eat on a cold, autumn day, while wearing a cosy, knitted jumper.

TIP If you don't eat all the stew, simply add in some vegetable stock and whizz until smooth in a blender for a fast soup the following day.

1 tbsp sunflower oil

1 onion, roughly chopped

100g (3½oz) rainbow chard, roughly chopped

3 cloves of garlic, crushed

Generous pinch of dried chilli flakes (red pepper flakes)

Pinch of ground cumin

Pinch of ground ginger

400g (14oz) can chopped tomatoes

4 rounded tbsp crunchy peanut butter

240g (8½oz) can red kidney beans, drained and rinsed

1 tbsp light soy sauce

Generous handful of fresh coriander (cilantro), roughly chopped

Pinch of sea salt

Heat the oil in a large pan over a high heat. Add the onion and rainbow chard to the pan and sauté for 2 minutes until the onion begins to soften.

Add the garlic to the pan, along with the chilli flakes, cumin and ginger and cook for a further minute.

Tip in the tomatoes and spoon in the peanut butter. Reduce the heat to medium.

Add the red kidney beans and soy sauce to the pan. Stir regularly to prevent burning and cook for 8 minutes.

Spoon into bowls and scatter with the coriander, then season with sea salt.

chickpea and chard korma

Serves 4 generously

This creamy, comforting korma is perfect served with clouds of basmati rice, or with warmed naan bread. Swiss chard offers a slight bitterness to the sweet and rich coconut milk base.

TIP Concentrated korma paste adds all of your favourite spices, with minimal effort. Check the ingredients to ensure the paste is dairy free.

1 tbsp sunflower oil

1 onion, finely chopped

2 cloves of garlic, crushed

4 large leaves of Swiss chard, stalks removed and roughly chopped

1 tsp ground cumin

½ tsp turmeric

1 tbsp korma paste (ensure dairy free)

400ml (14fl oz) can full-fat coconut milk

400g (14oz) can chickpeas, drained and rinsed

Pinch of sea salt

Small handful of fresh coriander (cilantro), roughly torn

Heat the oil in a large frying pan, add the onion and soften over a medium–high heat for 2–3 minutes. Add the garlic and Swiss chard, and sauté for a further minute.

Stir through the cumin and turmeric, then add the korma paste, coating the onion and Swiss chard.

Pour in the coconut milk and chickpeas, then allow to bubble for 10 minutes.

Season to taste with sea salt and scatter with the coriander.

fragrant cauliflower curry

Serves 2 generously

Cauliflower makes a fantastic curry ingredient, as its gentle flavour allows for all the spices to infuse through it, so every bite is as delicious as the next. This dish has a delicate blend of spices, which you can adjust to your own preferences.

TIP You can find cooked Puy lentils in ready-to-use packs available from most supermarkets, making them a super-speedy addition to this flavoursome curry.

2 tbsp sunflower oil

1 onion, finely chopped

1½ red fresh chillies: 1 finely chopped, ½ finely sliced

2cm (¾in) piece of ginger, peeled and minced

3 cloves of garlic, crushed

1 tsp ground turmeric

1 tsp garam masala

Pinch of ground cumin

400ml (14fl oz) can full-fat coconut milk

150ml (5fl oz/scant ⅔ cup) hot water

1 small cauliflower, cut into bite-size florets

2 large flatbreads (optional)

200g (7oz/1 cup) cooked Puy (French) lentils

Handful of fresh coriander (cilantro), roughly chopped

Generous pinch of sea salt

Heat the oil in a large pan over a medium heat. Add the onion, chopped red chilli and ginger to the pan and cook for 2–3 minutes until the onions soften but do not brown. Add the garlic, then stir through the turmeric, garam masala and cumin, cooking for a further minute.

Pour in the coconut milk and hot water and allow to simmer. Add the cauliflower to the pan and cook for 5–6 minutes, then increase the heat to medium–high until the cauliflower is al dente.

Grill the flatbreads, if using, for 1 minute on each side in a griddle pan.

Tip the lentils into the curry pan and stir through. Remove the pan from the heat and scatter with the coriander, sea salt and the sliced red chilli just before serving.

tea-infused chana masala

Serves 4

Allow chickpeas to be the star of the show in a fragrant, tea-infused sauce. Serve with warm naan breads and a spoonful of cooling vegan yogurt.

———

TIP Allow the tea to infuse in boiling water while you are cooking the onions, garlic and spices. Just remember to remove the loose leaves or tea bag before pouring the tea into the pan!

1 tbsp sunflower oil

2 onions, peeled and finely diced

2 cloves of garlic, peeled and finely sliced

2 tsp garam masala

Pinch of ground turmeric

Pinch of dried chilli flakes (red pepper flakes)

400g (14oz) can chopped tomatoes

2 x 400g (14oz) cans chickpeas, drained and rinsed

300ml (10½fl oz/1¼ cups) black tea

Generous pinch of sea salt flakes

Handful of coriander (cilantro) leaves, roughly torn

Juice of ½ unwaxed lemon

4 tbsp unsweetened soya yogurt

Heat the oil in a saucepan over a medium–high heat and cook the onions for 2 minutes until they begin to soften. Add the garlic, garam masala, ground turmeric and chilli flakes, then cook for a further 2 minutes, stirring frequently.

Pour in the chopped tomatoes, chickpeas and black tea, then cook for 10 minutes, stirring occasionally.

Remove from the heat and season with sea salt flakes. Scatter over the coriander leaves and squeeze over the lemon juice. Serve in bowls and spoon 1 tablespoon of yogurt over each.

moussaka bowls

Serves 4

I love the sweet, charred flavours of moussaka, but rarely have the time for the oven-baked version to be ready. These bowls contain all the flavours and textures of a slow-cooked moussaka, without the wait.

──────────

TIP Grilled courgette (zucchini) makes a great seasonal alternative to aubergine in this recipe.

For the lentils

1 tbsp olive oil

1 onion, finely chopped

1 clove of garlic, crushed

½ tsp ground cinnamon

½ tsp smoked paprika

½ tsp dried oregano

400g (14oz) can chopped tomatoes

400g (14oz) can green lentils, drained and rinsed

1 tsp yeast extract

For the aubergines

2 aubergines (eggplants), sliced into 1cm (½in) rounds

2 tsp olive oil

4 large tomatoes, halved

For the nutmeg yogurt and garnish

8 tbsp unsweetened soya yogurt

Pinch of freshly grated nutmeg

Pinch of sea salt flakes

Handful of fresh flat-leaf parsley, roughly torn

Start by making the lentils. Heat the olive oil in a large saucepan over a medium–high heat and cook the onion for 2–3 minutes until softened but not browned. Add the garlic, cinnamon, paprika and oregano, and cook for 1 minute, stirring constantly.

Pour in the chopped tomatoes, lentils and yeast extract, and simmer for 10 minutes.

In the meantime, prepare the aubergines. Heat a griddle pan until hot. Brush the aubergine slices with the olive oil and place them on the hot pan, cooking them for 2–3 minutes on each side until softened and grill marks appear. Grill the tomatoes for 1 minute, cut-side down.

Spoon the lentil mixture into bowls along with the griddled aubergine slices and tomato halves. Spoon over the soya yogurt and sprinkle with the grated nutmeg.

Season to taste with sea salt and scatter with the parsley.

aubergine, olive and butter bean cassoulet

Serves 4

Aubergine soaks up the wonderful flavours of oregano and cinnamon in this moreish cassoulet. Serve straight to the table in its cooking pot for a simple, rustic meal. A true crowd-pleaser.

––––––––

TIP Suitable for freezing.

2 tbsp olive oil

1 large aubergine (eggplant), cut into even bite-size cubes

1 tsp dried oregano

½ tsp ground cinnamon

1 red onion, finely diced

1 red (bell) pepper, sliced

400g (14oz) can chopped tomatoes

1 tbsp tomato ketchup

2 tbsp green olives

400g (14oz) can butter (lima) beans, drained and rinsed

Handful of fresh flat-leaf parsley, roughly chopped

Pinch of sea salt

Heat the oil in a large saucepan over a high heat, then add the aubergine, oregano and cinnamon. Cook for 3 minutes, stirring frequently.

Add the red onion and red pepper, and cook for a further 2 minutes, until the onion begins to soften.

Pour in the chopped tomatoes, 150ml (5fl oz/scant ⅔ cup) water and the ketchup, followed by the olives and butter beans. Reduce the heat to medium, partially cover with a lid and simmer for 10 minutes, stirring occasionally.

Scatter with the fresh parsley and season with sea salt just before serving.

chocolate chilli

Serves 4

This is soul food in a bowl. The fiery, fresh, dark and deep flavours marry together to create this indulgent chilli, which tastes like it's been cooking for hours. For those who are sceptical about the addition of cocoa, you'll find this dish has a beautifully balanced richness and a satisfyingly dark sauce.

TIP This chilli freezes perfectly, so whip up a batch, enjoy a portion and pop the rest in the freezer for evenings when you have less than 15 minutes to cook.

Also, be sure your chocolate is dairy free.

400g (14oz) can chopped tomatoes

1 onion, finely sliced

1 red (bell) pepper, deseeded and sliced

1 stick of celery, roughly chopped

4 tbsp frozen or canned sweetcorn

2 tsp cocoa powder

2 tsp mild chilli powder

1 tsp soft brown sugar

1 tsp smoked paprika

½ tsp ground cinnamon

400g (14oz) can red kidney beans, drained and rinsed

400g (14oz) can cannellini beans, drained and rinsed

1 spring onion (scallion), roughly chopped

Small handful of fresh coriander (cilantro), roughly torn

Juice of 1 unwaxed lime

1 square of dark (bittersweet) chocolate, grated

Add the chopped tomatoes and onion to a large saucepan over a medium–high heat. Throw in the red pepper slices, celery and sweetcorn, and cook for 2–3 minutes.

Spoon in the cocoa, chilli powder, sugar, smoked paprika and cinnamon. Stir through the kidney beans and cannellini beans until combined, and cook for 12 minutes, stirring frequently while the chilli bubbles away.

Remove from the heat and scatter with the spring onion, coriander and lime juice. Sprinkle over the dark chocolate just before serving.

fajita casserole crush

Serves 2

Cook this fun casserole in a stove-to-table dish and get everyone stuck in! Spoon through layers of crispy tortillas, smooth avocado and spicy beans and peppers.

TIP The base casserole is suitable for freezing, but top it with freshly baked tortillas before serving.

2 soft tortillas, cut into triangles

1 tbsp olive oil

1 tbsp sunflower oil

1 onion, roughly sliced

1 red (bell) pepper, sliced

1 yellow (bell) pepper, sliced

Small handful of green beans

1 tsp chilli powder

1 tsp smoked paprika

½ tsp garlic powder

½ tsp ground cumin

1 tsp yeast extract

400g (14oz) can red kidney beans, drained and rinsed

300g (10½oz/1¼ cups) passata (strained tomatoes)

6 cherry tomatoes, halved

1 avocado, finely chopped

1 small red onion, finely sliced

1 small green chilli, finely sliced

Juice of 1 unwaxed lime

Generous handful of coriander (cilantro), roughly torn

Generous pinch of smoked sea salt

Preheat the oven to 200°C/400°F/Gas 6.

Arrange the tortilla triangles on a baking tray and drizzle with the olive oil. Bake for 8–10 minutes until golden.

In the meantime, heat the sunflower oil in a large stove-to-table casserole dish over a medium–high heat and cook the onion and red and yellow peppers for 2–3 minutes until they begin to soften, then add the green beans, chilli powder, smoked paprika, garlic powder and cumin, and cook for a further minute.

Add the yeast extract, kidney beans and passata, and bubble for 10 minutes until the vegetables have softened.

Remove from the heat and scatter over the cherry tomatoes, avocado, red onion and green chilli. Squeeze over the lime juice.

Gently scatter with the baked tortilla chips and the coriander, and season with smoked sea salt to taste.

vegetable box pie with butter bean mash

Serves 2

This simple and delicious pie is designed to use up the stray vegetables at the bottom of your veg box or refrigerator. Toss them all into the herb-infused sauce, then layer over the creamy butter bean mash for a 15-minute main that will become a firm favourite. For the creamiest mash, source jarred butter beans instead of canned. If canned butter beans are your only option, soak them for a few minutes in boiling water to break down the skins.

TIP Chop the vegetables finely for the fastest cooking time, or slice through a food processor for extra-fast preparation.

For the filling

1 tbsp olive oil

1 small leek, finely chopped

2 carrots, finely chopped

1 celery stick, finely chopped

4 chestnut (cremini) mushrooms, chopped

Handful of chard leaves, chopped

2 cloves of garlic, crushed

a glug of red wine (ensure vegan)

½ tsp dried thyme

400g (14oz/1½ cups) passata (strained tomatoes)

Generous pinch of sea salt

For the butter bean mash

1 tbsp olive oil

1 clove of garlic, crushed

600g (1¼lb) butter (lima) beans, drained and rinsed

Juice of ½ an unwaxed lemon

Generous pinch of sea salt

Start by making the pie filling. Heat the oil in a pan over a medium heat. Add the leek, carrots and celery to the pan and soften for 2 minutes. Throw the mushrooms and chard into the pan and sauté for a further 2 minutes.

Add the garlic and pour in the red wine. Scatter over the thyme and reduce for 1 minute. Pour in the passata and add the salt, then loosely cover with a lid. Cook down for 10 minutes.

While the pie filling is cooking, prepare the butter bean mash. In a wide pan, heat the oil and cook the garlic over a low–medium heat for 1 minute. Add the butter beans to the pan and stir frequently for 3–4 minutes until the beans have heated through and are coated in olive oil and garlic.

Remove the butter bean pan from the heat and stir in the lemon juice. Mash down until semi-smooth, then season with sea salt.

Remove the other pan from the heat and divide the mixture into two pie dishes. Top with the butter bean mash and serve hot.

allotment cobbler

Serves 4

Homemade comfort
food at its best.

———

TIP The scone-dumplings
can be made up to 3 days
in advance when kept in a
sealed container.

For the scone-dumplings

160g (5¾oz/1¼ cups)
self-raising (self-rising) flour,
plus extra for dusting

Pinch of dried rosemary

Pinch of dried thyme

Generous pinch of salt

50g (1¾oz/3½ tbsp) vegan
butter

100ml (3½fl oz/scant ½ cup)
soya milk, plus extra for glazing

For the filling

1 tbsp olive oil

1 leek, finely chopped

1 medium courgette (zucchini),
cut into even chunks

1 red (bell) pepper, roughly
chopped

2 cloves of garlic, crushed

1 tsp dried oregano

1 tsp dried mixed herbs

400g (14oz) can chopped
tomatoes

4 rounded tbsp fresh broad
(fava) beans, podded

1 tbsp tomato ketchup

Juice of 1 unwaxed lemon

Preheat the oven to 220°C/
425°F/Gas 7. Line a baking
tray with baking paper.

Start by making the scone-
dumplings. In a bowl, mix
together the flour, rosemary,
thyme and salt, then rub in the
vegan butter until the mixture
resembles breadcrumbs. Stir
through the soya milk until
a smooth dough is created.
Use your hands to flatten the
dough to 2.5cm (1in) thick on
a lightly floured surface, then
use a scone cutter to make
8 scone-dumplings. Place them
onto the prepared baking tray
and brush with a little soya
milk. Bake for 10–11 minutes
until just golden.

In the meantime, make the
filling. In a large pot, heat
the olive oil over a medium
heat and cook the leek for
2 minutes. Add the courgette
and red pepper, cook for a
further 2 minutes, then throw
in the garlic, oregano and
mixed herbs, and cook for
1 minute more.

Add the chopped tomatoes,
broad beans and ketchup, and
cover with the lid. Bubble on
high for 7–8 minutes until the
vegetables are tender. Remove
the pot from the heat and
squeeze over the lemon juice.

Remove the scones from
the oven and carefully place
them over the cooked filling,
pressing them in gently to
absorb some sauce. Serve hot.

chestnut mushroom bourguignon

Serves 2 generously

Delight dinner guests with this deep, boozy, herbed bourguignon.

———

TIP Mushrooms absorb lots of liquid, so cook them in a separate pan to the base sauce to keep them at their best.

2 tbsp olive oil

600g (1lb 5oz) chestnut (cremini) mushrooms, brushed clean and halved

6 shallots, halved

1 carrot, sliced

1 clove of garlic, crushed

½ tsp dried thyme

½ tsp dried rosemary

3 tsp plain (all-purpose) flour

200ml (7fl oz/scant 1 cup) red wine (ensure vegan)

1 tbsp tomato ketchup

150ml (5fl oz/scant ⅔ cup) hot water

Pinch of sea salt and freshly ground black pepper

In a frying pan, heat 1 tablespoon of the olive oil and cook the mushrooms over a medium–high heat for 10 minutes until softened and fragrant.

In a separate large saucepan, heat the remaining olive oil and sauté the shallots and carrot over a medium–high heat for 4 minutes until the carrot begins to soften. Add the garlic, thyme and rosemary, and sauté for a further minute, then sprinkle in the flour and ensure the vegetables are well coated.

Pour the wine and ketchup into the shallot pan, stir through and allow to reduce for 10 minutes, adding the hot water when the sauce starts to thicken.

Spoon the cooked mushrooms and any juices into the saucepan and season to taste with sea salt and black pepper.

butternut squash and sage macaroni

Serves 2 generously

One of the most popular recipes on my website is a twice-baked butternut macaroni. It's also one of my favourite comfort foods. After having a craving for this slow-cooked dish, but being too hungry to wait, I recreated this creamy classic, which can be in your bowl within 15 minutes.

TIP To cook the butternut squash in the fastest time, ensure it is ripe and chopped into small, even pieces.

1 small butternut squash, peeled and chopped into small, even pieces

200g (7oz) dried macaroni (egg free)

1 tbsp olive oil

1 medium onion, finely chopped

2 cloves of garlic, crushed

2 tsp dried sage

400ml (14fl oz/1¾ cups) hot vegetable stock

Generous pinch of coarse sea salt and freshly ground black pepper

Small handful of fresh basil, to garnish

Bring a large saucepan of water to the boil. Carefully add the squash to the water and cook over a medium heat for 10–11 minutes until very soft, then drain.

Meanwhile, place the macaroni in a separate saucepan and cover with boiling water. Bring to the boil, then reduce the heat and simmer for 10 minutes until al dente. Drain and keep warm.

Heat the oil in a frying pan and add the onion and garlic. Sprinkle over the sage, then cook over a medium heat for 2–3 minutes until softened but not browned.

Spoon the onion, garlic and sage mixture into a blender or food processor, along with the butternut squash. Pour in the vegetable stock and blend on high until completely smooth.

Pour the smooth sauce over the macaroni and stir through thoroughly. Season with sea salt and black pepper and garnish with basil.

courgette and lemon pappardelle with pine nuts

Serves 2 generously

This fresh, lemony pasta tastes like summer in a bowl, even when it's cold outside. The grassy flavour of courgette meets the crisp bites of toasted pine nuts, all brought together by addictively slippery pappardelle ribbons.

TIP Use a good-quality extra virgin olive oil to dress the pasta, as a quick way to add a light flavour.

200g (7oz) dried pappardelle (egg free)

1 tbsp olive oil

1 onion, finely chopped

1 clove of garlic, crushed

2 medium courgettes (zucchini), grated

1 tbsp pine nuts

2 unwaxed lemons

Generous pinch of sea salt and freshly ground black pepper

2 tbsp extra virgin olive oil

Handful of fresh basil leaves

Cook the pappardelle in a large saucepan of boiling water over a medium–high heat for 10 minutes until al dente, then drain.

In the meantime, heat the olive oil in a large frying pan over a low–medium heat. Add the onion to the pan, followed by the garlic. Add the courgettes to the pan and increase the heat to medium. Stir frequently to avoid burning and encourage even cooking, and cook for 4–5 minutes. Add the pine nuts and cook for a further minute.

While the courgette is cooking, slice the lemons in half. When the courgettes have softened, squeeze over the juice of each lemon, through a sieve, then remove the pan from the heat and season with sea salt and black pepper.

Toss the cooked, drained pappardelle through the courgettes and coat evenly. Drizzle with the extra virgin olive oil and scatter over the basil. Serve immediately.

spaghetti
alla puttanesca

Serves 1 generously

I first came across this classic Italian dish in *Nigella's Kitchen* cookbook. Traditionally, the sauce contains anchovies; however, the olives and capers add all the saltiness it needs to be seasoned and addictive. All the ingredients are found in the store cupboard, making this the ultimate convenient, fast and seductive bowl of pasta.

TIP Switch spaghetti for your favourite egg-free pasta.

1 tbsp olive oil

2 cloves of garlic, crushed

½ tsp dried chilli flakes (red pepper flakes)

½ tsp dried oregano

2 tsp capers, drained of oil or brine

5 black olives, pitted and halved

250g (9oz/1 cup) passata (strained tomatoes)

1 tsp caster (superfine) sugar

100g (3½oz) dried spaghetti (ensure egg free)

Sea salt and freshly ground black pepper

Heat the olive oil in a large saucepan over a medium heat and cook the garlic for 1 minute until softened. Sprinkle in the chilli flakes and oregano, along with the capers and olives, and allow them to infuse in the oil for a further minute.

Pour in the passata and stir through the sugar to balance the acidity. Loosely cover with a lid and allow to simmer for 10 minutes.

In the meantime, cook the spaghetti in boiling water in a separate pan for 9–10 minutes until al dente.

Drain the water from the pan and toss the spaghetti through the sauce until coated. Remove from the heat and season with sea salt and black pepper to taste. Serve immediately.

risotto caprese

Serves 1 generously

The magical results of this less-than-15-minute risotto are created in a pressure cooker. In what can take up to 30 minutes of cooking and laborious stirring, risotto can be high maintenance and definitely not a recipe for a 15-minute time slot – until you've tried this recipe. There's no peeking allowed once the pressure is set, so ensure your liquid volumes are exact in this trusted recipe.

TIP Vegan cream cheese can be found in many supermarkets and health-food shops. Experiment with plain, herbed or chilli-flavoured varieties!

If you don't have a pressure cooker, simmer the risotto down for 30 minutes, stirring frequently until creamy.

2 tbsp olive oil

1 onion, finely chopped

1 tsp dried oregano

100g (3½oz/½ cup) arborio rice

100ml (3½fl oz/scant ½ cup) white wine (ensure vegan)

200ml (7fl oz/scant 1 cup) hot vegetable stock

6 soft sundried tomatoes, drained of oil and roughly chopped

4 cherry tomatoes, halved

4 black olives, pitted and halved

6 tsp vegan cream cheese

Generous handful of fresh basil leaves, torn

Pinch of sea salt and freshly ground black pepper

Add the olive oil and onion to a pressure cooker over a medium–high heat, and soften the onion for 2–3 minutes, without the lid on at this stage.

Add the dried oregano and rice, and coat fully in the onion mixture until the edges of the rice become transparent. Stir constantly.

Pour in the wine and simmer for 2–3 minutes until absorbed.

Pour in the vegetable stock and stir through, then close the lid on the pressure cooker. Bring the pan up to high pressure and cook for 5 minutes, then release the pressure quickly, as per the manufacturer's instructions.

Reduce the heat to low and stir through the sundried tomatoes, cherry tomatoes and black olives, heating them through for 1 minute.

Serve in a large bowl and spoon over the vegan cream cheese, pushing teaspoon-sized amounts of the cheese into the rice and allowing it to gently melt through.

Scatter with the basil leaves and season with sea salt and black pepper to taste.

garden crumble

Serves 4

Empty your vegetable drawer into this hearty meal that friends and family will love. If you've never tried a savoury crumble before, you're in for a treat!

TIP Adding chopped walnuts to the topping gives extra crunch and a toasted flavour. It also works well with pumpkin seeds, sunflower seeds and mixed chopped nuts.

1 tbsp sunflower oil

1 onion, peeled and roughly chopped

1 clove of garlic, peeled and crushed

1 medium courgette (zucchini), diced

1 red (bell) pepper, sliced

6 cherry tomatoes, halved

10 green beans, sliced

1 tsp herbes de Provence

1 tsp dried rosemary

400g (14oz) can chopped tomatoes

Generous pinch of sea salt flakes and freshly ground black pepper

For the crumble topping
100g (3½oz/¾ cup) plain (all-purpose) flour

50g (1¾oz/½ cup) rolled oats

2 tbsp shelled walnuts, roughly chopped

2 tbsp vegan butter

Zest of 1 unwaxed lemon

Preheat the oven to 200°C/400°F/Gas 6.

Heat the oil in a large saucepan over a medium–high heat and cook the onion for 2 minutes until softened. Add the garlic, courgette, red pepper, cherry tomatoes and green beans and sprinkle in the herbes de Provence and rosemary. Cook for a further 2 minutes, then tip in the chopped tomatoes, and season with the sea salt and black pepper. Simmer for 10 minutes.

In the meantime, make the crumble topping. Mix the flour, oats and walnuts in a bowl, then rub in the vegan butter until the mixture resembles breadcrumbs. Stir through the lemon zest, then spoon evenly onto a baking sheet. Bake for 8–9 minutes until golden.

Spoon the vegetable mixture into a serving dish, then sprinkle over the crumble topping just before serving.

SWEET
STUFF

plum and almond galette

Serves 4

Traditionally, a galette is a free-form pastry pie, slow-baked with a fruity filling. Its rustic, home-baked appearance and piping hot fruit topping is an effortless yet impressive addition to any family table. Who'd have thought it could be recreated in just 15 minutes? Your secret is safe with me.

TIP Many brands of store-bought pastry are accidentally vegan as they use vegetable fat instead of dairy butter, but always check the ingredients before buying.

1 sheet of store-bought shortcrust pastry (ensure vegan)

6 ripe plums

2 tbsp plum jam (jelly)

1 tbsp amaretto liqueur

2 tbsp flaked (slivered) almonds

Preheat the oven to 220°C/425°F/Gas 7.

Unroll the pastry directly onto a baking tray. Fold over the edges roughly, sealing with a little water if needed. Bake for 10–12 minutes until golden.

In the meantime, prepare the plum filling. Slice each plum in half, remove the stone, then cut each half into four thin slices. Place the sliced plums into a pan with the jam and amaretto liqueur and bring to the boil over a medium–high heat for 5–6 minutes until bubbling.

In a separate dry pan, toast the almonds over a high heat for 1–2 minutes until golden brown.

Remove the pastry from the oven and carefully spoon in the plum and amaretto filling. Sprinkle over the toasted almonds and serve immediately.

traditional sultana scones

Makes about 6 medium scones

Quintessentially British and perfect with a pot of tea, there's little in life that can beat a sultana scone. This recipe is perfect for when unexpected guests turn up, as they are simple to make and quick to cook – and best served warm, straight from the oven.

_____

TIP When using a dough cutter, never twist when removing it as it will result in uneven scones. Simply press down firmly and remove with the dough intact – simple and quick!

220g (8oz/1¾ cups) self-raising (self-rising) flour, plus extra for dusting

1 tsp baking powder

2 tbsp caster (superfine) sugar

50g (1¾oz) vegan butter, plus extra for greasing

50g (1¾oz/⅓ cup) sultanas (golden raisins)

120ml (4fl oz/½ cup) soya milk, plus extra for brushing

Preheat the oven to 220°C/425°F/Gas 7.

In a large mixing bowl, stir together the flour, baking powder and sugar. Rub in the vegan butter until the mixture resembles breadcrumbs. Stir in the sultanas until coated with flour. Pour in the milk, a little at a time, and work into a smooth dough.

Place the dough on a floured surface. Use your hands to press it out to a 2cm (¾in) thickness. Using a scone cutter, press through the dough and place the scones onto a greased baking tray. Brush the top of each scone with soya milk.

Bake for 10–11 minutes until the tops of the scones are golden. Best served warm.

Serve with lashings of jam and fresh fruit.

raspberry, rose and pistachio crumble

Serves 4

Crumble is my ultimate pudding. The sweet, baked fruit and crunchy topping makes it the most comforting bowl there is. Always bake the fruit in a separate tray to the topping, then assemble just before serving; that way the crumble topping will stay crunchy and crisp.

TIP Soft fruits cook in super-fast time, so when you're trying different flavour combinations, opt for fast-cook fruits, including clementines, blackberries, rhubarb and blackcurrants.

300g (10½oz/2½ cups) fresh raspberries

1 tsp good-quality rose extract

For the topping
100g (3½oz/¾ cup) plain (all-purpose) flour

50g (1¾oz/½ cup) rolled oats

50g (1¾oz/¼ cup) demerara sugar

2 tbsp coconut oil or vegan butter, at room temperature

2 tbsp shelled pistachios

Preheat the oven to 200°C/400°F/Gas 6.

Arrange the raspberries on a baking tray and drizzle over the rose extract.

To make the topping, mix together the flour, oats, and sugar in a bowl. Rub in the coconut oil or vegan butter until the mixture resembles breadcrumbs. Roughly chop the pistachios in half and stir into the mixture. Spoon the topping mixture into a separate deep baking tray.

Bake both trays for 10–12 minutes until the fruit is soft and bubbling and the topping is golden. Spoon the fruit into bowls and top generously with the crumble.

peanut butter blondie flapjacks

Makes 6

These squidgy, oaty bars are halfway between a blondie and a brownie, with the comforting taste of creamy peanut butter. Add a pinch of coarse sea salt to the top just before baking as an easy way to take these blondie flapjacks from simple to sublime.

———

TIP For a delicious dessert, crumble some (still warm) flapjack over your favourite vegan ice cream.

100g (3½oz/½ cup) light brown sugar

2 tbsp vegan butter

6 tbsp smooth peanut butter

3 tbsp golden syrup

300g (10½oz/3 cups) rolled oats

Pinch of coarse sea salt

Preheat the oven to 180°C/350°F/Gas 4.

Add the sugar, vegan butter, peanut butter and golden syrup to a medium saucepan and melt over a medium–high heat for 2–3 minutes. Stir often until the butter has melted and all the ingredients have combined. Tip in the oats and stir until all the oats have been coated in the melted mixture.

Press the oaty mixture into a 3cm (1¼in) depth baking tray lined with baking paper and flatten down using the back of a spoon. Crush over the sea salt and bake for 10 minutes until golden.

Remove from the oven and cut into squares. Leave in the baking tray until cool.

cherry pot pies

Makes 4

Dark, juicy cherries are sweet, sticky and zesty in these golden pastry-topped pies. Pitted cherries are a useful ingredient to keep in the freezer for fruity pies or for whipping into smoothies when the fruit is out of season. These pies are topped with puff pastry for a rustic taste of home.

——————

TIP Many brands of store-bought puff pastry use vegetable oils instead of butter, making it accidentally vegan. Always check the ingredients.

1 sheet of pre-rolled puff pastry (ensure dairy-free)

1 tsp soya milk, for glazing

300g (10½oz/1¾ cups) frozen or fresh pitted cherries

Juice of 1 unwaxed lemon

2 tbsp caster (superfine) sugar

Sprinkle of icing (confectioners') sugar

Preheat the oven to 200°C/400°F/Gas 6.

Place four ramekin pots over the pastry and cut around them with a knife. Place the rounds of pastry onto a non-stick baking tray and brush the tops with a little soya milk. Bake for 10–12 minutes until golden and nicely puffed.

In the meantime, add the cherries, lemon juice and caster sugar to a pan and bring to a bubble over a medium heat, stirring frequently for 10 minutes until the sugar has dissolved and created a dark sauce.

Spoon the cherries and sticky sauce into the ramekins.

Remove the pastry lids from the oven and carefully place them on top of the cherry filling. Sprinkle over a little icing sugar. Serve hot.

carrot cake flapjacks

Makes about 8 squares

When visiting my favourite vegan bakery, I find it difficult to choose between a slice of carrot cake and a square of chewy flapjack (it's not unheard of for me to buy both). When I'm not able to visit the bakery, I bake carrot cake flapjacks and remember why I love these treats so much.

TIP Use golden syrup and sunflower oil to reduce the cooking time of these flapjacks, as you don't have to spend additional time melting vegan butter and dissolving granulated sugar.

4 tbsp sunflower oil

4 rounded tbsp golden syrup

1 tsp ground cinnamon

½ tsp ground nutmeg

150g (5½oz/1½ cups) rolled oats

1 tbsp raisins

1 tbsp chopped walnuts

1 carrot, roughly grated

Preheat the oven to 200°C/400°F/Gas 6.

Line a 30 x 20cm (12 x 8in) baking tray that's 3cm (1¼in) deep with baking paper.

In a large mixing bowl, mix together the sunflower oil, golden syrup, cinnamon and nutmeg until combined.

Tip in the oats, raisins and walnuts, and stir vigorously to coat in the syrup mixture, then stir through the carrot.

Press the mixture into the prepared baking tray, using the back of a spoon to smooth the top. Bake for 12 minutes, then allow to cool in the tin before slicing into even squares. The flapjacks will become firmer and chewy when cool.

sesame brittle thins

Makes 1 tray

I love to snack on those little sesame snacks from the supermarket, but they don't come cheap. This two-ingredient recipe is simple, quick and fuss-free.

TIP These sweet thins will last for up to 5 days in an airtight container.

½ tsp sunflower oil, for greasing

5 tbsp sesame seeds

200g (7oz/1 cup) caster (superfine) sugar

Rub the oil lightly onto a baking tray to prevent the brittle sticking.

Add the sesame seeds to a frying pan and toast over a low–medium heat for 2–3 minutes until golden, then transfer to a bowl and set aside.

Return the pan to the heat and sprinkle in the sugar. Leave for 5 minutes without stirring, until bubbling and light golden.

Stir in the toasted sesame seeds and remove from the heat.

Pour a thin layer onto the prepared baking tray. Leave in a cool place for 5 minutes to set.

To break, cut into squares with a sharp knife, or make shards by dropping the baking tray onto a worktop.

two-minute chocolate chip and pecan cookie

Makes 1

Yes, you read that correctly! You will have this comforting cookie in just 2 minutes. Like any cookie, it will harden as it cools; however, if you want a warm, soft-centre cookie eat it immediately. Or feel free to wait 5 minutes until the edges crisp a little. I think it's incredible served with a scoop of non-dairy vanilla ice cream.

TIP Many supermarkets sell dark chocolate chips that are accidentally vegan. If you don't have any to hand, chop up two squares of a dark (bittersweet) chocolate bar to use in place of the chocolate chips.

1 rounded tbsp vegan butter

2 tbsp soft brown sugar

1 tsp vanilla extract

1 tbsp pecan nuts

4 tbsp plain (all-purpose) flour

1 tbsp dark (bittersweet) chocolate chips

In a microwave-safe bowl, spoon in the vegan butter and melt in an 850W microwave for 30 seconds.

Stir the brown sugar, vanilla extract, pecan nuts and flour into the melted vegan butter to form a dough, then stir through the chocolate chips.

Spoon the mixture as a single cookie onto a microwave-safe plate, then microwave for 1 minute 30 seconds until cooked.

turkish delight melt-in-the-middle mug cake

Makes 1

When the need for indulgent chocolate cake arises, this 2-minute mug cake satisfies on every level. You'll spoon through soft, warm cake before you reach a sweet, gooey centre. You're welcome.

TIP Serve with a scoop of vegan ice cream, if you like

2 tbsp self-raising (self-rising) flour

2 tbsp cocoa powder

2 tbsp caster (superfine) sugar

1 tbsp sunflower oil

¼ tsp rose extract

2 squares of Turkish delight (ensure gelatine free and carmine free)

In a large mug, mix together the flour, cocoa powder and sugar until combined.

Pour in the sunflower oil, 3 tablespoons of cold water and the rose extract, then whisk with a fork until combined and smooth.

Press 1 square of Turkish delight into the centre of the mug until it is completely covered in batter.

Cook in a 800W microwave for 2 minutes and allow to cool for 1 minute before topping with the other square of Turkish delight and digging in.

coffee-poached figs with orange and hazelnuts

Serves 2

This is one of my favourite autumnal desserts, when figs are in season and at their best. After a hearty casserole or pie, a light pudding like this works a treat.

TIP Serve with a spoonful of smooth vanilla soya yogurt to contrast with the hot, poached figs.

4 fresh figs, washed

500ml (17½fl oz/2 cups) strong black coffee

1 tbsp soft brown sugar

2 whole cardamom pods

Pinch of ground cinnamon

Zest of 1 unwaxed orange

Generous handful of blanched hazelnuts, roughly chopped

Place the figs in a deep saucepan and pour in the coffee.

Spoon in the sugar, cardamom pods, cinnamon, and half of the orange zest, then simmer over a medium heat for 8–9 minutes until the figs are tender and the coffee sauce thickens slightly.

In the meantime, toast the chopped hazelnuts in a frying pan for 2–3 minutes until just golden.

Serve the poached figs in bowls, and ladle over a little of the coffee poaching sauce. Sprinkle over the toasted hazelnuts and the remaining orange zest.

peanut butter melt-in-the-middle chocolate pudding

Serves 4 generously

Unexpected dinner guest? Mix up this decadent dessert in mere moments.

––––––––

TIP Serve with a generous scoop of vegan ice cream.

For the peanut butter filling

3 rounded tbsp smooth peanut butter

100ml (3½fl oz/scant ½ cup) hot water

For the chocolate pudding

4 tbsp self-raising (self-rising) flour

2 tbsp cocoa powder

2 tbsp granulated sugar

2 tbsp sunflower oil

Start by making the peanut butter filling. Use a fork to whisk together the peanut butter and hot water until combined and smooth.

For the chocolate pudding, mix together the flour, cocoa powder and sugar in a small, heatproof bowl. Spoon in the oil with 6 tablespoons of cold water and stir until combined.

Spoon out 1 rounded tablespoon of the cake mixture and pour the peanut butter filling into the resultant hole. Smooth over the removed cake mixture, covering any visible peanut butter.

Cook in an 850W microwave for 3 minutes, then allow to stand for 1 minute. Serve hot.

lime and coconut syllabub

Serves 2 generously

This simple, five-ingredient syllabub is rich and creamy with a hint of zesty lime. Serve chilled in glasses for the perfect minimalist dessert.

TIP Chilling a can of coconut milk will separate the cream from the water, so you can simply scoop out the cream to make the most delicious desserts.

400ml (14fl oz) can full-fat coconut milk, chilled

4 tbsp coconut yogurt

2 tbsp maple syrup

2 unwaxed limes

1 tsp toasted coconut chips

Open the can of chilled coconut milk and scoop out the solid cream, discarding the remaining coconut water (or reserve it for another recipe). Spoon the coconut cream into a mixing bowl and add the coconut yogurt, then the maple syrup. Use an electric whisk to whip the cream, yogurt and syrup together for about 5 minutes until gentle peaks begin to form.

In the meantime, finely grate the zest of the limes, then halve one of the limes, ready for juicing.

Stir the lime zest through the creamy mixture (reserving a teaspoon for serving), then squeeze in the juice of ½ lime.

Spoon into dessert glasses and top with a few toasted coconut chips and the reserved lime zest to serve.

salted chocolate mousse

Serves 4

Imagine an intensely rich mousse, silky smooth with a subtle balance of sweetness and smoked salt. Serve at the end of an exquisite meal, in a bright white espresso cup. Just don't tell anyone it contains avocado.

――――

TIP No avocado? Use 200g (7oz) of silken tofu instead.

250g (9oz) good-quality very dark (bittersweet) chocolate

1 ripe avocado

3 tbsp maple syrup

2 tbsp unsweetened soya milk

1 tsp vanilla extract

Pinch of smoked sea salt flakes

Break up the chocolate into even pieces and place in a heatproof bowl. Blast for 30 seconds in the microwave, stir, then heat again for a few more seconds until melted.

Cut the avocado in half, remove the stone and scoop out the flesh into a blender. Spoon in the melted chocolate, maple syrup, soya milk and vanilla extract and blend on high until combined. Use a spatula to scrape the mixture back to the centre of the blades and blend on high again until completely smooth.

Pour into small cups or ramekins, then sprinkle with the smoked sea salt. Chill for 5 minutes before serving.

instant
mango fro-yo

Serves 2 generously

When I lived in the city, I loved eating a tub of frozen yogurt on a hot day. I was lucky to find a wonderful shop (that I passed on my way home from work throughout summer) that sold a vegan version. No matter where you are, stopping and having a moment of calm is good for the mind and body; this instant fro-yo will transport you to somewhere tropical.

200g (7oz) frozen mango chunks

5 rounded tbsp coconut yogurt

Juice of 1 unwaxed lime

Add the frozen mango, coconut yogurt and lime juice to a high-powered blender and blitz until smooth and creamy. Serve immediately, with a sprinkling of lime zest grated over the top, if you like.

TIP Frozen mango chunks are available in large supermarkets. Stock up and use them in curries, smoothies and puddings.

the lazy millionaire's shortbread pudding

Serves 6

Millionaire's shortbread is a baked classic. This quick recipe was created when I planned to bake a batch for guests, but ran out of time. So I pressed the shortbread base into individual ramekins and served it at the table with hot caramel sauce and melted chocolate, for my guests to create themselves. It was a huge success! I know you are going to love it too.

TIP The caramel sauce can be chilled and used as a dipping sauce. I love it with banana and pineapple, or vegan marshmallows!

For the shortbread biscuit base

50g (1¾oz/scant ½ cup) plain (all-purpose) flour

1 tbsp caster (superfine) sugar

Pinch of fine sea salt

30g (1oz) vegan butter

For the caramel sauce

3 tbsp soft brown sugar

2 tbsp golden syrup

1 rounded tbsp vegan butter

1 tsp vanilla extract

150ml (5fl oz/scant ⅔ cup) soya cream

For the chocolate sauce

200g (7oz) good-quality very dark (bittersweet) chocolate

100ml (3½fl oz/scant ½ cup) soya cream

Preheat the oven to 190°C/375°F/Gas 5.

Start by making the biscuit base. Combine the flour, sugar and sea salt in a food processor, then add the vegan butter and mix until a dough is formed. Press the dough into 6 ramekins, in a 2cm (¾in) layer. Bake for 9–10 minutes until pale golden.

While the bases are cooking, make the caramel sauce. Put the sugar, golden syrup, vegan butter and vanilla extract in a pan. Simmer over a medium heat for 4–5 minutes without stirring. Remove from the heat and allow to cool for 1 minute, then whisk in the soya cream. Pour into a jug (pitcher) and keep warm.

For the chocolate sauce, break up the chocolate into a heatproof bowl and blast in the microwave for 20 seconds, stir, then blast for 20 seconds more, or until fully melted. Whisk in the soya cream, then transfer into another jug and keep warm.

Remove the ramekins from the oven and serve immediately for a softer, cakier base, or allow to cool for a few minutes for a firmer base. Serve with the caramel and chocolate sauces and pour both into the ramekins just before enjoying while hot.

pink lemonade

Makes about 1 litre (1¾ pints/4½ cups)

This homemade lemonade makes me think of picnics with wicker baskets, gingham cloths and cucumber sandwiches. Whether you're going on a picnic or simply in need of a sweet drink, this pink lemonade is refreshing, zingy and beautifully cloudy.

TIP Store-bought pink lemonade may be coloured with carmine, which is a pink-red pigment obtained from a species of insect. Carmine can also be listed as cochineal or E120, and this additive isn't suitable for vegans.

Zest and juice of 6 unwaxed lemons

200g (7oz/1 cup) caster (superfine) sugar

100g (3½oz/¾ cup) raspberries

1 litre (1¾ pints/4½ cups) chilled water

Ice cubes, for serving

Add the lemon zest and juice, sugar and raspberries to a saucepan and bring to a simmer over a medium heat for 5 minutes until the sugar has dissolved.

Remove from the heat and pour in the chilled water.

Strain the lemonade into a jug (pitcher) and discard the cooked ingredients.

Serve the lemonade in ice-filled glasses.

chocolate pretzel freakshake

Serves 1

Why choose between something sweet or salted when you can have both? Just get freakshaking!

TIP Many flavours and brands of vegan ice cream are available in supermarkets and health-food shops. Try them all and decide on your favourite!

4 squares of dark (bittersweet) chocolate (ensure dairy free)

200ml (7fl oz/scant 1 cup) chilled chocolate soya milk

2 tsp smooth peanut butter

1 scoop of vegan chocolate ice cream

1 scoop of vegan vanilla ice cream

6 small salted pretzels

Small handful of salted popcorn

Heat the dark chocolate for 2–3 minutes in a heatproof bowl over a pan of simmering water until melted.

In the meantime, whisk together the chocolate soya milk and peanut butter in a wide-necked jug (pitcher) until combined, then pour into a tall glass or jar.

Spoon over the chocolate and vanilla ice creams.

Use a spoon to drizzle over some of the melted chocolate onto the ice cream.

Press on the pretzels and popcorn, and drizzle with the remaining melted chocolate.

peanut butter cheesecake shots

Serves 4

Smooth peanut butter makes for the most silken, smooth filling in these cheesecake shots. Best served in small glasses or shot glasses, because they are so rich.

––––––

TIP Many supermarket own-brand digestive biscuits don't contain cow's milk, but always check the ingredients.

3 tbsp smooth peanut butter, at room temperature

100ml (3½fl oz/scant ½ cup) soya single (light) cream

1 rounded tbsp vegan butter

6 digestive biscuits (graham crackers); ensure dairy free

4 tsp dark (bittersweet) chocolate chips (ensure dairy free)

Soften the peanut butter in a bowl, then pour in the soya cream and use a fork or balloon whisk to beat to a thick, creamy consistency.

In a small saucepan, melt the vegan butter over a low heat while you break the biscuits into a breadcrumb consistency, either using a food processor, blender or by adding them to a food bag and beating with a rolling pin. Remove the pan from the heat, then pour the biscuit crumbs into the pan and stir to combine.

Allow the biscuit mixture to cool for a few minutes, then press into the bottom of small glasses. Spoon in the peanut butter mixture and finish with a sprinkle of chocolate chips. The cheesecake shots can be refrigerated for 2 hours before serving for a gently chilled dessert.

white chocolate fondue

Serves 2

Who doesn't love silky, melted chocolate? Use bright berries and vegan marshmallows to dip into this luxurious sweet fondue.

————

TIP Vegan white chocolate can be found in the free-from sections of most supermarkets, or in health-food shops. Vegan white chocolate buttons work well in this recipe, too!

For the fondue

200g (7oz) vegan white chocolate, broken into pieces

200ml (7fl oz/scant 1 cup) soya single (light) cream

1 vanilla pod (bean)

To serve

6 blackberries

6 cherries

6 strawberries

6 vegan marshmallows (ensure gelatine and carmine free)

To make the fondue, add the white chocolate and soya cream to a heatproof bowl. Halve the vanilla pod lengthways, then scrape the seeds into the bowl.

Bring a small saucepan of water to a simmer, then set the bowl over the pan to create a bain-marie. Stir occasionally for 5–6 minutes until the chocolate has melted and combines with the cream.

Pour into a fondue bowl and keep warm with a tea light.

Serve with blackberries, cherries, strawberries and vegan marshmallows to dip.

chocolate ganache churros

Serves 2 generously

Spanish-style churros are the ultimate sweet finger-food, perfect for dipping into a thick, chocolate ganache. The quantity of the ganache is generous, so you can relax the double-dipping rules.

TIP There's no need to buy a churro maker as it's so simple to cook them at home the traditional way

For the churros
2 tbsp sunflower oil, plus 800ml (28fl oz/3½ cups) for frying

3 tbsp caster (superfine) sugar

½ tsp fine salt

125g (4½oz/1 cup) plain (all-purpose) flour

For the dusting
2 tbsp caster (superfine) sugar

½ tsp ground cinnamon

For the chocolate ganache
200g (7oz) dark (bittersweet) chocolate, broken into pieces (ensure dairy free)

150ml (5fl oz/scant ⅔ cup) thick coconut cream

Start by making the churros. Add 250ml (8¾fl oz/1 cup) of cold water, the 2 tablespoons of sunflower oil, the sugar and salt to a saucepan and bring to a simmer over a medium heat. Tip in the flour and beat until a firm ball of dough is formed.

Heat the sunflower oil for frying in a deep-fat fryer or a heavy-bottomed pan until it reaches 180°C (350°F) and a small piece of the dough turns golden within 1 minute. While the oil is warming up, place the dough in a large piping bag fitted with a star-shaped nozzle (tip).

Squeeze 8cm (3¼in) pieces of dough into the hot oil, using clean scissors to cut each from the nozzle. In batches, cook the churros for 2–3 minutes until golden. When golden, transfer to a plate lined with paper towels and keep warm.

For the dusting, mix together the sugar and cinnamon on a plate, then roll the cooked churros in to coat.

To make the ganache, add the chocolate to a heatproof bowl and place over a pan of simmering water, stirring for 3–4 minutes until melted. Stir the melted chocolate into the coconut cream, then stir through until fully combined.

Serve the warm churros alongside bowls of chocolate ganache for dipping.

easter egg hot chocolate

Serves 2

Having excess chocolate around the house after Easter celebrations is never a bad thing, especially when you can whip up this decadent hot chocolate. Delicately spiced and lifted with freshly squeezed orange juice, treat yourself to a cosy drink that is so much better than any store-bought variety.

TIP Light brown sugar gives a caramel flavour to this drink, but it can be substituted with granulated white sugar for simple sweetness.

400ml (14fl oz/scant 1¾ cups) sweetened soya milk

100g (3½oz) dark (bittersweet) chocolate (ensure dairy free), broken into even pieces

1 tsp light brown sugar

Juice of ½ unwaxed orange

Pinch of ground cinnamon

Pinch of ground nutmeg

Heat the soya milk, chocolate and sugar in a large saucepan over a low–medium heat, whisking for 4–5 minutes until the chocolate has melted.

Next, whisk in the orange juice, cinnamon and nutmeg until gently frothy.

Pour into mugs and serve hot.

marshmallow fluff

Makes 1 jar

Do you ever longingly look at jars of pillowy marshmallow fluff and dream about spooning it over pancakes or loading it onto cupcakes? Well this recipe is the answer. It uses a product called aquafaba, which is the water from a can of chickpeas, and has long been used as an egg substitute. It's often used in vegan meringues, mousses, mayonnaise – and this sweet marshmallow fluff.

_____

TIP Cream of tartar can be found in supermarket baking aisles.

60g (2oz/½ cup) icing (confectioners') sugar

Unsalted water drained from 400g (14oz) can chickpeas (reserve the chickpeas for another recipe)

½ tsp cream of tartar

1 tsp vanilla extract

Add the icing sugar and chickpea water to a stand mixer bowl and whisk on high for 5 minutes.

Add the cream of tartar and vanilla extract, and whisk for a further 10 minutes until whipped and creamy.

lemon curd

Makes 1 medium jar

Creamy, zesty lemon curd, generously spread onto white bread, brings back memories of childhood summers spent in the garden. I always have a small jar of this in the refrigerator – I hope you will too.

TIP Traditionally, lemon curd is made using eggs and butter. This vegan version sets as it cools; however, I love it straight from the pan, drizzled onto hot toast or over a vanilla cake. If you prefer a more set version, pour into a clean jar and leave overnight in the refrigerator.

Zest and juice of 2 unwaxed lemons

150g (5½oz/¾ cup) granulated sugar

400ml (14fl oz/scant 1¾ cups) sweetened soya milk

1 level tbsp cornflour (cornstarch)

1 tbsp vegan butter

Add the lemon zest and juice, sugar, soya milk and cornflour to a pan, and bring to the boil over a medium–high heat. Simmer for 10 minutes, stirring frequently.

Stir through the vegan butter and cook for a further 2 minutes until the curd is smooth and glossy.

Use as a thickened drizzle while warm, or allow to cool and pour into a jar to set overnight. It will keep in the refrigerator for up to a week.

miso caramel sauce

Makes 1 small jar

Meet salted caramel's sophisticated big sister. White miso adds a salty, umami depth to a sweet, smooth caramel sauce. Serve hot with pancakes or use as a dipping sauce when cooled.

———

TIP Miso is a natural flavouring made from fermented soya beans. It adds depth to sweet and savoury dishes, and lasts well in the refrigerator.

3 tbsp soft brown sugar

2 rounded tbsp golden syrup

1 rounded tbsp vegan butter

1 tsp vanilla extract

1 tsp white miso paste

200ml (7fl oz/scant 1 cup) soya single (light) cream

Melt the sugar, golden syrup, vegan butter, vanilla extract and miso paste in a saucepan over a low heat for 5–6 minutes without stirring.

Remove from the heat and allow to cool for a few minutes, then whisk in the soya cream until silken and smooth.

SNACKS
AND
SIDES

sumac onion salad

Serves 4

Sumac has a fresh, citrus flavour and is a traditional ingredient in Middle-Eastern cuisine. I think it tastes more like lemon than lemon itself! Serve with falafel, houmous and flatbreads.

——————

TIP For less sharpness in the onions, pour over enough hot water to cover the onions, then stand for 5 minutes before draining away the water.

1 red onion

1 white onion

1 tsp ground sumac

Generous handful of fresh flat-leaf parsley, finely chopped

4–5 fresh mint leaves, finely chopped

1 unwaxed lemon

1 tbsp extra virgin olive oil

Pinch of sea salt

Finely slice both the onions. Add to a bowl and sprinkle with the sumac.

Stir the parsley and mint through the onions.

Halve the lemon and squeeze in the juice through a sieve. Pour in the olive oil and stir to combine.

Allow the salad to infuse for 10 minutes, then season with sea salt.

grilled courgettes with dill yogurt

Serves 4

This plate of hot, charred courgettes is a versatile side dish, but also works well as a large salad plate when served over crisp leaves. Keep the yogurt chilled until serving to best appreciate the contrast between the hot courgettes and the cool, herbed yogurt.

TIP Heat the griddle pan over a high heat while you prepare the courgettes to achieve the optimum grilling temperature.

4 medium courgettes (zucchini), sliced into long 2cm (¾in) thick strips

Drizzle of extra virgin olive oil

4 rounded tbsp unsweetened soya yogurt

1 tbsp fresh dill, finely chopped

Juice of ½ unwaxed lemon

Pinch of sea salt

1 tsp capers, drained of brine or oil

Heat a griddle pan over a high heat while you brush the courgette strips with olive oil. Place the strips onto the hot pan and cook for 3–4 minutes until defined char lines begin to show. Flip the courgettes over and cook on the other side for 3–4 minutes.

In the meantime, make the yogurt dressing. Combine the soya yogurt, dill, lemon juice and sea salt in a small bowl, and chill until ready to serve.

When the courgettes are grilled on both sides, arrange them on a serving plate and scatter with the capers. Generously spoon over the yogurt dressing just before serving.

mint and mustard green beans

Serves 4

Brighten up your dinner table with these fresh and flavourful green beans.

———————

TIP This hot side dish also tastes excellent as a chilled salad.

400g (14oz) green beans, ends trimmed

4 tbsp extra virgin olive oil

Juice of 1 unwaxed lemon

1 tsp Dijon mustard

Generous handful of fresh mint leaves, finely chopped

Bring a saucepan of water to the boil over a high heat and throw in the green beans. Cook for 4–5 minutes until tender.

Meanwhile, whisk together the olive oil, lemon juice and mustard until combined.

Drain the water from the green beans and pour over the dressing. Toss until all the green beans are coated.

Scatter with the mint leaves just before serving.

tenderstem broccoli with orange and chilli

Serves 2

Purple sprouting broccoli and sugar snap peas are stir-fried with freshly squeezed orange juice, hot chilli and crushed nuts in this side dish that packs a flavour punch. You'll find pre-chopped nuts in health-food shops and some supermarkets, or make your own by whizzing a handful of mixed nuts in a food processor.

TIP As a side dish, this recipe serves two people. Serve it up for one with some noodles for a quick yet substantial lunch.

1 tbsp sunflower oil

8 stems of long-stem broccoli, stalk ends trimmed

Handful of sugar snap peas

Pinch of dried chilli flakes (red pepper flakes)

1 unwaxed orange

1 tbsp mixed chopped nuts

Handful of fresh coriander (cilantro), roughly chopped

Heat the oil in a wok until hot.

Throw the broccoli into the hot wok along with the sugar snap peas and chilli flakes, and stir-fry on high for 5 minutes.

Slice the orange in half and squeeze over half the juice through a sieve, reserving the other half of the orange for another recipe. Add the nuts and stir through for 1 minute.

Remove from the heat and scatter with the coriander just before serving.

red cabbage and apple slaw

Serves 4

This slaw has the right balance of sweet and sharp, making it the perfect accompaniment to just about anything.

—————

TIP You'll find apple cider vinegar near the oils and dressings in most major supermarkets and local health-food shops.

300g (10½oz) red cabbage, coarsely shredded

2 Granny Smith apples, grated

3 spring onions (scallions), finely chopped

1 tbsp apple juice

2 tsp apple cider vinegar

1 tsp Dijon mustard

Place the shredded cabbage in a large bowl.

Combine the apples and spring onions with the cabbage.

Spoon in the apple juice, apple cider vinegar and mustard, then stir through to combine.

bombay potatoes

Serves 4

Here's a 15-minute spin on Bombay potatoes that makes them quick and effortless to make. Don't be afraid to use canned potatoes here – they've already been peeled, saving you time, and they absorb the flavours of the spices perfectly.

TIP Thoroughly drain and rinse the potatoes before use.

3 tbsp sunflower oil

1 tsp mustard seeds

1 tsp turmeric

½ tsp chilli powder

½ tsp paprika

300g (10½oz) can new potatoes, drained, rinsed and halved

6 ripe tomatoes, quartered

1 green chilli, deseeded and finely sliced

Small handful of fresh coriander (cilantro), roughly chopped

Pinch of sea salt

Heat the oil in a frying pan over a medium–high heat for 2 minutes, then fry the mustard seeds until they start to brown. Stir in the turmeric, chilli powder and paprika until combined into a hot, flavoured oil.

Carefully stir in the potatoes and coat in the oil. Cook for 5 minutes until the potatoes are hot, then remove from the heat.

Stir through the tomatoes and green chilli to coat in the oil mixture, then scatter with the coriander and sea salt just before serving.

skin-on seaside chips

Serves 2

I couldn't write this book without including my favourite comfort food: chips. Let this recipe transport you to the great British seaside, tucking into a bag of hot, vinegary chips by the sea.

TIP Leaving the skin on the potatoes adds extra flavour, as well as making them quicker to prepare. Simply scrub thoroughly before use.

500ml (17½fl oz/2 cups) sunflower oil, for frying

2 large Maris Piper potatoes, chopped into chunky chips (fries)

Generous sprinkle of malt vinegar

Pinch of sea salt flakes

Heat the oil in a deep-fat fryer to 130°C (265°F). If you don't have a deep-fat fryer, use a heavy-bottomed saucepan to heat the oil over a medium heat until a test chip sizzles and floats to the top.

Use a slotted spoon to carefully add the potatoes to the oil. Fry for 8 minutes until starting to turn golden, then remove and set aside.

Increase the heat of the deep-fat fryer 190°C (375°F), or if you're using a heavy-bottomed saucepan, increase the heat to high.

Carefully place the par-cooked chips back into the pan for a further 4–5 minutes until golden brown.

Serve while hot, sprinkled with malt vinegar and sea salt.

cauliflower and dill mash

Serves 2

When you're in a hurry, mashed potato is out of the question. However, if you simply swap potato for cauliflower, and blitz it with some creamy ingredients, you can soon enjoy that comforting taste in under 15 minutes. You will find non-dairy cream cheese in many large supermarkets, with many stocking more than one brand.

TIP If you don't have time to get mashing, simply pop all the ingredients into a food processor and blitz until smooth.

1 cauliflower

½ tbsp fresh dill, finely chopped

3 tbsp non-dairy cream cheese

Pinch of sea salt and freshly ground black pepper

Bring a pan of water to the boil while you remove the stem of the cauliflower. Chop into florets, then add to the water and boil for 10 minutes until completely softened.

Thoroughly drain the water and add the dill and cream cheese to the pan. Mash the cauliflower until smooth and creamy, then season with salt and black pepper.

parsley and butter bean mash

Serves 4

Lemony, herby butter beans make the most perfect mash, and best of all, it's ready in under 10 minutes.

——————

TIP Bring the lemon to room temperature before use, so it becomes easier to juice.

2 x 400g (14oz) cans butter (lima) beans, drained and rinsed

Generous handful of fresh flat-leaf parsley, finely chopped

Generous drizzle of extra virgin olive oil

Juice of 1 unwaxed lemon

Pinch of sea salt

Tip the butter beans into a saucepan. Cover with boiling water and simmer for 5 minutes, then drain and rinse in boiling water.

Stir through the parsley, olive oil and lemon juice, then use a potato masher to mash the beans until smooth.

Season with sea salt to taste.

garlic baguettes

Serves 4

It's often difficult to source vegan garlic bread in the supermarket, as many contain dairy. This is a simple recipe using store-bought, part-baked baguettes and a homemade garlic butter.

——————

TIP Score the baguettes with a knife, leaving space at the bottom – that way the bread remains whole until it is shared at the table.

4 tbsp vegan butter, softened

2 cloves of garlic, crushed

Small handful of flat-leaf parsley, finely chopped

½ tsp sea salt flakes, crushed

2 part-baked white baguettes, scored into 8 slices for tearing

Drizzle of extra virgin olive oil

Preheat the oven to 200°C/400°F/Gas 6.

In a mixing bowl, combine the vegan butter, garlic, parsley and sea salt flakes until creamy.

Arrange the scored baguettes onto a baking tray, then use a teaspoon to push small amounts of the vegan butter between the slices of bread.

Wrap the baguettes in foil and bake for 5 minutes, then fold back the foil carefully and bake for another 4–5 minutes until golden. Drizzle with extra virgin olive oil and serve hot.

refried beans

Serves 4

I love this Tex-Mex classic – proper comfort food.

───────

TIP These refried beans will keep in the refrigerator for up to 3 days.

1 tbsp sunflower oil

1 red onion, finely sliced

1 tsp chipotle paste

1 tsp paprika

½ tsp ground cinnamon

½ tsp garlic powder

400g (14oz) can borlotti beans, drained and rinsed

400g (14oz) can black beans, drained and rinsed

Juice of ½ unwaxed lime

Generous pinch of smoked sea salt

Heat the sunflower oil in a large saucepan over a medium–high heat and cook the onion for 3 minutes until softened. Add the chipotle paste, paprika, cinnamon and garlic powder, and stir through for 1 minute.

Tip in the borlotti beans and black beans, and reduce the heat to low–medium, stirring frequently for 8 minutes.

When the beans are hot, use a potato masher to crush them a little. Squeeze over the lime juice and season with smoked sea salt. Serve hot.

parsnip fritters

Serves 4

When you have a couple of parsnips left over from making a roast dinner, grate them into these family-friendly fritters that little fingers will love.

TIP Serve with cranberry sauce for dipping.

6 tbsp sunflower oil

120g (4½oz/generous ¾ cup) plain (all-purpose) flour

1 tsp baking powder

1 tsp dried mixed herbs

Generous pinch of black pepper

½ tsp fine sea salt

2 medium parsnips, peeled and grated

Start heating the oil in a frying pan over a medium heat while you make the batter.

In a large bowl, mix together the flour, baking powder, mixed herbs, black pepper and sea salt. Stir in the grated parsnip, ensuring it's coated in the flour mixture. Pour in 100ml (3½fl oz/scant ½ cup) of cold water and stir to form a batter.

Add tablespoon-sized portions of batter to the pan and cook for 2–3 minutes on each side until golden. Serve hot.

carrot fries with cinnamon salt

Serves 2 generously

These 'fries' are actually oven baked, making them a healthier, cheaper alternative to potato fries. You'll love the subtle hint of sweetness from the cinnamon.

———

TIP Preheat the oven as you're peeling and chopping the carrots into batons to ensure it's hot and ready to cook the fries in the fastest time.

6 carrots, peeled and cut into 1 x 5cm (½ x 2in) batons

4 tbsp sunflower oil

½ tsp fine sea salt

Pinch of ground cinnamon

Preheat the oven to 220°C/425°F/Gas 7.

Arrange the carrot batons in a single layer on two baking trays, then rub over the oil.

Bake for 13–14 minutes until softened.

In the meantime, mix together the sea salt and cinnamon.

Remove the carrot fries from the oven and scatter liberally with the cinnamon salt. Serve hot alongside the Fiery butternut squash ketchup (page 298).

chilli salt tortilla chips

Serves 2 generously

These crispy chips are the perfect weekend snack and a great way to use up tortillas.

TIP These tortilla chips will last up to 3 days when kept in a sealed container.

2 soft tortillas

2 tbsp olive oil

½ tsp dried chilli flakes (red pepper flakes)

½ tsp smoked salt flakes

Preheat the oven to 180°C/350°F/Gas 4.

Slice the tortillas into triangles and arrange in a single layer on a baking tray, or use two if needed.

Drizzle over the oil and gently rub onto the triangles.

Sprinkle over the chilli flakes and smoked salt, then bake for 5–6 minutes until the edges are golden and crisp.

paprika-roasted crispy kale

Serves 2 generously

I love this crispy kale served with Pad Thai jay with lime and sesame (page 148), although it makes a pretty good snack on its own too.

TIP Buy a bag of pre-shredded kale to roast, to save time chopping the larger leaves.

1 tbsp olive oil

½ tsp paprika

Pinch of sea salt flakes

200g (7oz) kale, shredded

Preheat the oven to 180°C/350°F/Gas 4.

Mix the oil, paprika and salt in a bowl. Add in the kale and gently coat in the oil mix.

Place the kale onto a baking sheet in a single layer without overlapping so it cooks evenly. Bake for 7 minutes, then remove the tray and shake to distribute the oil, then bake for another 2 minutes until crisp.

naan chips

Serves 4

Hot, crispy and moreish, these naan chips are the perfect dipping partners to the Coconut, cucumber and garden mint raita (page 285).

—

TIP Read the ingredients of store-bought naan breads, as they may contain dairy products. Many supermarket-own brands are made without dairy.

2 naan breads (ensure vegan), cut into triangles

½ tsp dried chilli flakes (red pepper flakes)

Generous drizzle of olive oil

Pinch of smoked sea salt

Preheat the oven to 200°C/400°F/Gas 6.

Place the naan triangles onto a baking tray, scatter with the chilli flakes and drizzle with olive oil.

Bake for 8–10 minutes until golden and crisp. Scatter with smoked sea salt just before serving.

salt and vinegar potato peel crisps

Serves 2

Instead of mindlessly throwing away those potato peelings, use them to bake these moreish crisps. I love salt-and-vinegar-flavoured snacks, but you can mix it up by adding smoked paprika, chilli powder or garam masala. Load into a bowl and enjoy, or store in an airtight container for up to 3 days.

TIP Thinner peelings result in crisper snacks, so use a vegetable peeler for the crunchiest crisps. Thicker peelings may need a longer cooking time.

Peelings of 4 thoroughly washed large potatoes

3 tbsp sunflower oil

Sprinkle of malt vinegar

Generous pinch of fine sea salt

Preheat the oven to 200°C/400°F/Gas 6.

Arrange the potato peelings on a baking tray and drizzle over the oil. Use your hands to rub the oil over all surfaces of the peelings.

Sprinkle with malt vinegar, then bake for 10 minutes until golden and crisp.

Remove from the oven and season with sea salt.

beer-battered onion rings

Serves 4

These pub-style onion rings make a great sharing starter using store-cupboard ingredients.

TIP If you don't have beer available, sparkling water makes a similarly light batter, with a less malted flavour.

500ml (17½fl oz/2 cups) sunflower oil, for frying

150g (5½oz/generous 1 cup) self-raising (self-rising) flour

160ml (5½fl oz/⅔ cup) beer (ensure vegan)

2 large onions, peeled, finely sliced and separated into rings

Heat the oil in a large frying pan over a low–medium heat while you prepare the batter.

In a large bowl, whisk together the flour and beer to form a smooth batter.

Working in batches so you don't overcrowd the pan, dip the rings of onion into the batter, then use tongs to carefully drop them into the hot oil. Cook for 3–4 minutes, or until golden. Carefully remove with tongs or a slotted spoon, then drain on paper towels. Serve hot.

pan-fried
crispy chickpeas

Serves 4

These crispy chickpeas are a delicious snack any time of the day.

———

TIP The cooked chickpeas will last for up to 4 days in an airtight container.

4 tbsp olive oil

400g (14oz) can chickpeas, drained and rinsed

1 tbsp smoked paprika

1 tsp dried chilli flakes (red pepper flakes)

½ tsp ground cumin

Pinch of sea salt

Heat the olive oil in a large frying pan over a medium heat and cook the chickpeas for 10 minutes until they start to become crispy.

Scatter over the smoked paprika, chilli flakes, cumin and sea salt, and stir through for 2 minutes.

Remove from the heat and allow to cool for a couple of minutes before serving.

green tea and coconut rice

Serves 4

Serve clouds of this creamy, fragrant rice alongside roasted veggies or your favourite curry.

——————

TIP White basmati rice cooks quicker than brown rice, making it the fastest option for this dish

200g (7oz/scant 1 cup) creamed coconut

350g (12oz/2 cups) basmati rice

600ml (20fl oz/2½ cups) green tea made with boiling water and a tea bag, or tea leaves discarded after brewing

Pinch of sea salt

Heat the creamed coconut in a saucepan over a medium heat, then add the rice and stir through to coat the grains.

Pour in the hot green tea, stir and loosely cover with a lid. Cook for 10–12 minutes until the liquid has been absorbed and the rice is plump. Season with sea salt to taste.

saffron rice

Serves 1

Vibrant and precious, saffron infuses the basmati rice to give a flowery, honeyed fragrance with a gently sweet, spiced flavour.

TIP Saffron is expensive; however, you only need a very small amount each time you use it and it keeps well in a cool, dark cupboard.

If you don't have saffron available, use a pinch of ground turmeric instead.

100g (3½oz/½ cup) basmati rice, rinsed

Pinch of saffron threads

1 cinnamon stick

2 cardamom pods

1 star anise

1 tsp plump sultanas (golden raisins)

1 tsp pistachios, shelled and halved

Drizzle of extra virgin olive oil

Pinch of sea salt

Add the rice, saffron threads, cinnamon stick, cardamom pods and star anise to a saucepan with 250ml (8¾fl oz/1 cup) of cold water, and bring to the boil over a high heat. Reduce the heat and simmer for 12–13 minutes until the liquid has been absorbed.

Remove the cinnamon stick, cardamom pods and star anise and discard. Add the sultanas and pistachios and stir to combine.

Drizzle with extra virgin olive oil and season with sea salt to taste.

ESSENTIALS

guacamole

Serves 2 generously

Guacamole should be chunky, rustic and full of flavour. Mash the ingredients with a fork and get your hands involved to combine this traditional Mexican side dish.

TIP There's no need to peel and chop the avocado; simply use a spoon to scoop out the ripe flesh.

1 large tomato, finely chopped

1 small red onion, finely chopped

½ small red chilli, deseeded and finely chopped

2 ripe avocados

Generous handful of fresh coriander (cilantro), roughly chopped

1 unwaxed lime

Generous pinch of sea salt flakes

Put the tomato, onion and chilli into a bowl.

Halve the avocados and spoon out the flesh into the bowl, then mash all the ingredients together.

Mix the coriander into the guacamole. Slice the lime in half and squeeze the juice through a sieve into the bowl before stirring through. Season with sea salt to serve.

{pictured overleaf}

tomato, red onion and coriander salsa

Serves 4

Fresh, homemade salsa is not only delicious but simple to prepare. Serve as a dip or load inside a sandwich for a fiery filling.

TIP This salsa will keep for up to 3 days in the refrigerator.

300g (10½oz) ripe tomatoes, chopped

1 red onion, finely chopped

1 red chilli, deseeded and finely sliced

Handful of fresh coriander (cilantro), torn

1 unwaxed lime

Pinch of sea salt

Place the tomatoes, onion, chilli and coriander in a bowl.

Cut the lime in half, then squeeze in the juice through a sieve. Sprinkle over the sea salt and stir to combine all the ingredients.

{pictured overleaf}

beetroot guacamole

Serves 4

Give guacamole a colourful twist with beetroot. Earthy, chunky and perfect for sharing.

———

TIP Cooked beetroot can be found in supermarket salad refrigerators, which saves on long roasting times.

2 ripe avocados, peeled and stones removed

1 spring onion (scallion), finely sliced

2 small cooked beetroots (beets), diced

Generous handful of fresh coriander (cilantro), finely chopped

Juice of 1 unwaxed lime

Generous pinch of smoked sea salt

In a bowl, use a fork to crush the ripe avocado flesh until semi-smooth.

Stir through the spring onion, beetroots and coriander, then stir through the lime juice. Season with salt to taste.

If you prefer a silky smooth dip, blitz all of the ingredients in a blender.

lemon and almond pesto

Serves 2

I always have a jar of this moreish pesto in the refrigerator as it's so delicious and versatile. Stir it through pasta, spoon over bruschetta, or use as a dip for breadsticks.

TIP This pesto will keep for up to 5 days in the refrigerator.

1 clove of garlic, peeled

30g (1oz) fresh basil leaves, torn

50g (1¾oz/generous ½ cup) flaked (slivered) almonds

1 unwaxed lemon

150ml (5fl oz/scant ⅔ cup) good-quality extra virgin olive oil

Pinch of sea salt

Put the garlic and basil into a blender or food processor with the flaked almonds.

Grate the zest of the lemon into the mix, then halve the lemon and squeeze in the juice through a sieve.

Pour in the oil, then blitz until almost smooth. Season with sea salt.

olive tapenade

Serves 2

Whether it's an accompaniment to a sliced baguette and a glass of wine, or part of a tapas dinner, this tapenade will have everyone dreaming of summer.

——————

TIP This is delicious served with the stuffed Ramiro peppers on page 133.

200g (7oz/2 cups) pitted mixed olives

1 tbsp capers, rinsed

1 unwaxed lemon

4 tbsp good-quality extra virgin olive oil

Add the olives and capers to a food processor.

Cut the lemon in half and squeeze in the juice through a sieve.

Pour in the oil and blitz until semi-smooth.

sundried tomato pesto

Makes 1 small jar

Try this rich and flavourful pesto stirred through pasta or on bruschetta for added flavour. It's a vibrant twist on classic green pesto.

———

TIP No need to drain the oil from the sundried tomatoes before using; the extra oil helps to create a smooth pesto.

2 tbsp pine nuts

1 clove of garlic, peeled

Generous pinch of sea salt

250g (9oz/2¼ cups) soft sundried tomatoes in oil

Generous handful of fresh flat-leaf parsley, torn

150ml (5fl oz/scant ⅔ cup) good-quality extra virgin olive oil

Pulse together the pine nuts, garlic and sea salt in a blender until crushed.

Add the sundried tomatoes, parsley and extra virgin olive oil, and blend until almost smooth.

This pesto will keep for up to 3 days in an airtight container in the refrigerator.

broccoli pesto

Makes 1 small jar

Boost your pesto with the addition of broccoli! It will also stretch the pesto further to make it a wonderful pasta sauce to serve four. If you don't have a food processor or blender, you can finely chop or grate all the ingredients before mixing into a coarse pesto.

TIP Don't waste the broccoli stalk – chop it and add it to a stir-fry for a fresh, crunchy addition.

Suitable for freezing.

1 tbsp flaked (slivered) almonds

1 large broccoli, cut into florets

1 small handful of basil, including the stalks

Juice of ½ unwaxed lemon

1 clove of garlic, peeled

4 tbsp extra virgin olive oil

½ tsp sea salt

In a dry frying pan, toast the flaked almonds over a high heat for 2 minutes until golden, then tip them into a food processor or blender.

Add the broccoli florets, basil, lemon juice, garlic and olive oil and blitz to a coarse paste. Stir through the sea salt.

caramelized red onion houmous

Serves 2 generously

Once you try this, you'll never choose store-bought houmous again. Invest in a good-quality tahini, which is creamy rather than set. Chickpeas that are jarred rather than canned are easier to whip into houmous, and they also provide a smoother texture. Serve with warmed pita breads.

——————

TIP This houmous will keep in the refrigerator for up to 3 days.

1 tbsp olive oil

1 red onion, finely sliced

600g (1¼lb) canned chickpeas, drained and rinsed

2 cloves of garlic, crushed

3 tbsp good-quality tahini

1 unwaxed lemon

Pinch of ground cumin

Pinch of za'atar

Generous drizzle of extra virgin olive oil

Heat the olive oil in a pan over a low–medium heat. Add the onion to the pan and slowly cook down for 8 minutes.

Tip the chickpeas into a bowl. Cover with boiling water and allow to sit while the onion is cooking. This process will make a smoother houmous.

Add the garlic to the onion pan and cook for a further 2 minutes, until the onion is starting to brown.

Tip half the onion and garlic mixture into a blender, along with the tahini. Drain the hot water from the chickpeas and add to the blender. Chop the lemon in half and squeeze in the juice through a sieve. Blend until smooth.

Stir through the remaining onion and garlic mixture along with the ground cumin and za'atar. Drizzle over the extra virgin olive oil just before serving.

green pea houmous

Serves 2

Tender and fresh peas add a new taste to houmous. Serve with crudités or toasted pita bread.

─────────

TIP Tahini, or sesame seed paste, can be found in the supermarket world food aisle or in Middle Eastern shops.

200g (7oz/1½ cups) frozen or fresh peas

Juice of 1 unwaxed lime

½ tsp ground cumin

Generous handful of fresh coriander (cilantro)

2 tbsp tahini

Generous glug of extra virgin olive oil

Generous pinch of sea salt

Simmer the peas in boiling water for 2 minutes until heated through, then drain thoroughly.

Add the peas, lime juice, cumin, coriander and tahini to a high-powered blender and blitz until smooth.

Spoon out into a bowl and stir through the extra virgin olive oil. Season to taste with salt.

butter bean houmous

Serves 2 generously

If you like your houmous creamy and whipped, switch chickpeas for budget-friendly butter beans in this twist on the classic dip.

TIP Smooth peanut butter makes a great substitute for tahini (sesame seed paste) if you don't have any available. Just add a little extra oil at the blending stage.

400g (14oz) can butter (lima) beans, drained and rinsed

2 tbsp tahini

Juice of 1 unwaxed lemon

6 tbsp extra virgin olive oil

1 clove of garlic, peeled

Pinch of sea salt

Generous handful of flat-leaf parsley, finely chopped

Place the butter beans, tahini and lemon juice in a food processor or blender jug and blitz until semi-smooth.

Add 5 tablespoons of the olive oil, the garlic and sea salt, and blitz again until smooth.

Stir the flat-leaf parsley through the houmous, along with the remaining tablespoon of olive oil.

trio of dips

Serves 1

When you need a taster of everything, these dips will cool, excite and zing up your chip game.

————————

TIP Egg-free vegan mayo is readily available in supermarket free-from sections, as well as health-food shops.

For the maple and soy dip
2 tbsp maple syrup

1 tbsp dark soy sauce

2–3 drops vegan Worcestershire sauce (ensure anchovy free)

For the lemon mayo dip
Zest of ½ unwaxed lemon

2 tbsp vegan mayonnaise

1 tbsp lemon juice

Pinch of sea salt

For the spicy tomato dip
3 tbsp tomato ketchup

½ tsp harissa paste

2–3 drops hot sauce

For the maple and soy dip:
Whisk together the maple syrup, soy sauce and Worcestershire sauce and pour into a small serving bowl.

For the lemon mayo dip:
Finely grate the lemon zest into the vegan mayonnaise and squeeze in the lemon juice. Combine fully and season with sea salt to taste.

For the spicy tomato dip:
Mix together the ketchup, harissa and hot sauce until combined. Pour into a small serving dish.

coconut, cucumber and garden mint raita

Serves 4

Cooling and refreshing, this raita is a vital addition to any Indian-inspired meal and delicious served with Naan chips (page 255).

TIP You can find many brands and varieties of coconut yogurt in supermarkets and health-food shops. I'd recommend choosing an unsweetened version for this recipe.

8 tbsp chilled unsweetened coconut yogurt

¼ cucumber, finely chopped

Handful of mint leaves, finely chopped

Juice of 1 unwaxed lime

Pinch of sea salt

Spoon the coconut yogurt into a large bowl.

Stir in the cucumber, mint and lime juice, and season with sea salt to taste.

four-ingredient soured cream with chives

Makes 1 small pot

Load this vegan soured cream over Tortilla tacos (page 142), for a tangy flavour experience.

———

TIP Opt for unsweetened, plain soya yogurt for this recipe. You can use the rest to make a curry extra creamy, or make your own flavoured sweet yogurt with fruits you have available.

8 tbsp unsweetened soya yogurt

Juice of ¼ unwaxed lemon

Pinch of sea salt

Small handful of chives, finely chopped

In a bowl, whisk together the soya yogurt and lemon juice until combined. Refrigerate for 10 minutes.

Sprinkle in the sea salt and whisk again, then stir through the chives to serve.

pomegranate, cucumber and mint relish

Serves 2 generously

Refreshing and cooling, this simple relish is lovely served with a tagine.

———

TIP To make pomegranate seed removal easy, massage the skin of the fruit before slicing it in half, then firmly tap the seeds into a bowl.

1 pomegranate

10cm (4in) piece of cucumber

5–6 fresh mint leaves, finely chopped

Slice the pomegranate in half and tap out the juicy seeds.

Chop the cucumber into small chunks. Add it to the pomegranate along with the mint and stir to combine.

mango, radish and lime salsa

Serves 4

Sweet, fresh and the perfect accompaniment to any spiced dish.

——————

TIP This salsa will keep for 2–3 days in an airtight container in the refrigerator.

1 medium mango, peeled and chopped into small chunks

6 radishes, quartered

Handful of fresh flat-leaf parsley

Juice of 1 unwaxed lime

Combine the mango, radishes and parsley in a bowl. Squeeze over the lime juice and allow to stand for 10 minutes before serving.

cucumber salsa

Serves 4

Load this into a baguette with hot, roasted vegetables for a perfect lunch.

TIP Revive a cucumber that looks past its best in this zingy salsa.

½ cucumber, finely diced

2 spring onions (scallions), finely sliced

1 red chilli, deseeded and finely sliced

Zest and juice of ½ unwaxed lime

Handful of flat-leaf parsley, finely chopped

Drizzle of extra virgin olive oil

Pinch of sea salt flakes

Combine the cucumber, spring onions, chilli and lime zest in a bowl.

Squeeze in the lime juice, then stir through the parsley. Allow to chill for 10 minutes.

Stir through the oil and sea salt flakes just before serving.

sweetcorn salsa

Serves 4

This two-step salsa brightens up any table! Serve with tortilla chips or veggie chilli, or load into Chilli bean sliders (page 121).

TIP Smoked salt adds a subtle layer of flavour to the salsa, but if you don't have any available, regular sea salt works fine.

325g (11oz) canned sweetcorn, drained and rinsed

1 red (bell) pepper, deseeded and finely diced

1 small red onion, peeled and finely chopped

2 tomatoes, deseeded and chopped

Handful of coriander (cilantro), finely chopped

Small handful of flat-leaf parsley, finely chopped

Juice of 1 unwaxed lime

Generous pinch of smoked sea salt flakes

In a bowl, combine the sweetcorn, red pepper, red onion, tomatoes, coriander and parsley.

Squeeze over the lime juice and season with smoked salt.

blackberry salsa

Makes 1 small jar

This dark and interesting salsa is perfect to serve alongside an autumnal Sunday lunch.

————

TIP Fresh blackberries offer the most complex flavours, but frozen blackberries also work well; simply defrost fully before using.

150g (5½oz/1¼ cups) blackberries

1 small green chilli, deseeded and finely chopped

Small handful of fresh coriander (cilantro), finely chopped

Zest and juice of 1 unwaxed lime

1 tsp maple syrup

Pinch of sea salt

In a mixing bowl, roughly mash the blackberries to release the juices.

Stir in the chilli, coriander, lime zest and juice, and the maple syrup.

Season to taste with sea salt. This salsa will keep for 3–4 days in an airtight container in the refrigerator.

grapefruit gremolata

Makes 1 small bowl

As winter becomes spring, brighten up slow-cooked dishes such as tagines and Bolognese with a sprinkle of gremolata. It's zesty, fresh and unexpected with bitter grapefruit.

TIP Switch grapefruit for unwaxed lemon or orange for an easy flavour twist.

Small handful of fresh flat-leaf parsley, finely chopped

2 cloves of garlic, grated

Zest of 1 unwaxed grapefruit, coarsely grated

Combine all the ingredients in a bowl and allow the flavours to infuse for at least 10 minutes before serving.

smoky tomato pan-chutney

Serves 2

Some dishes just call out for a tangy side of tomato chutney and my version cooks in just 10 minutes. I love serving it warm.

TIP Worcestershire sauce adds a splash of spices in an instant. Although, some Worcestershire sauce brands contain anchovies, so be sure that you use a sauce that is suitable for vegans.

8 ripe red tomatoes, finely chopped

2 tsp vegan Worcestershire sauce

½ tsp caster (superfine) sugar

½ tsp smoked paprika

2–3 drops of hot chilli sauce

Add the tomatoes to a pan, along with their seeds and juice, and 5 tablespoons of cold water.

Add the Worcestershire sauce, sugar, smoked paprika and hot chilli sauce.

Cook over a medium–high heat for 10 minutes, breaking up the tomato chunks as you stir. Serve warm.

quick pickled radishes

Serves 4

I love the tang of these pickled radishes that cut through the creaminess of coconut-based curries. No one will ever believe they're ready to eat in less than 15 minutes!

TIP Rice vinegar has a mild flavour, but if you prefer something that packs a tangy punch, switch to cider vinegar.

10 radishes, very finely sliced

1 spring onion (scallion), finely sliced

5 tbsp rice vinegar

1 tsp maple syrup

Pinch of dried chilli flakes (red pepper flakes)

Small handful of fresh coriander (cilantro), finely chopped

Pinch of sea salt

Put the sliced radishes and spring onion into a small jar or small bowl.

Spoon over the rice vinegar and maple syrup, then stir in the chilli flakes, coriander and sea salt. Allow to infuse for 10 minutes before serving.

two-minute bbq mayonnaise

Makes 1 small pot

No need to buy expensive flavoured mayonnaise when you have all the ingredients in the cupboard already! Once exclusive to health-food shops, egg-free mayonnaise is now available in most supermarkets, usually in the free-from aisle.

———

TIP Serve as a dip with Beer-battered onion rings (page 259).

6 tbsp egg-free mayonnaise (ensure vegan)

2 tbsp BBQ sauce (ensure vegan)

3–4 drops of Tabasco sauce

Juice of ¼ unwaxed lime

Small handful of chives, finely chopped

Add the vegan mayonnaise, BBQ sauce, Tabasco sauce and lime juice to a bowl and whisk until combined.

Stir through the chopped chives and serve.

beetroot ketchup

Serves 4 generously

This vivid pink beetroot ketchup is a flavour twist on a classic ketchup, which is wonderful served with my Vegetable box pie with butter bean mash (see page 170).

─────

TIP This ketchup will keep for up to 5 days in the refrigerator.

300g (10½oz) cooked beetroot (beet), roughly chopped

1 tbsp malt vinegar

Pinch of dried thyme

Pinch of ground nutmeg

2 tbsp extra virgin olive oil

Add the beetroot to a pan along with any excess beetroot juice.

Stir in the vinegar, thyme and ground nutmeg and cook for 10 minutes over a medium heat.

Remove from the heat and tip the mixture into a blender. Pour in the oil and whizz until smooth and puréed.

fiery butternut squash ketchup

Makes 1 small pot

As each butternut squash can vary in size, it can be easy to end up with excess roasted butternut squash. Use leftover roasted squash to make this delicious ketchup, which tastes great with Carrot fries with cinnamon salt (page 252).

──────────

TIP Harissa is a hot, aromatic spice paste made using chillies, spices, herbs and a little rose water. It is available in most supermarkets and Middle Eastern shops, and keeps for months in the refrigerator. Use it to add flavour to tagines, soups and houmous for plenty of heat with little effort.

For the perfect roasted butternut squash, drizzle sunflower oil over the peeled veg, season with salt and pepper, then roast at 200°C/400°F/Gas 6 for 35–40 minutes, turning once.

Suitable for freezing.

150g (5½oz) leftover roasted butternut squash

1 tsp harissa paste

Juice of ¼ unwaxed lemon

Pinch of sea salt flakes

2 tsp plain soya yogurt

Add the roasted butternut squash, harissa paste, lemon juice and sea salt with 100ml (3½fl oz/scant ½ cup) of cold water to a blender, or blend in a bowl with a hand blender and blitz until smooth.

Swirl through the soya yogurt and serve as a dip.

chilli and ginger stir-fry sauce

Serves 4

Save a little money on store-bought stir-fry sauces by creating this five-ingredient sauce. Simply add your chosen vegetables to the wok after making the sauce, for a quick, budget-friendly meal. For added protein, throw in some cashew nuts, peanuts, frozen edamame (soya) beans or sesame seeds.

TIP Store ginger root whole and peeled in the freezer and grate the amount you need from frozen to avoid waste and keep the flavour vibrant.

2 tbsp sunflower oil

1 tsp dried red chilli flakes (red pepper flakes)

2cm (¾in) piece of ginger, peeled and grated

4 tbsp light soy sauce

Juice of 1 unwaxed lime

Heat the oil in a large wok over a high heat for 1 minute.

Add the chilli flakes and ginger and stir-fry for 2 minutes, then spoon in the soy sauce and cook for a further minute.

Drizzle over the lime juice after you've added the main bulk of the stir-fry (vegetables and vegan protein of your choice) to avoid any bitterness during cooking.

sweet chilli sauce

Makes 1 large jar

I buy bags of chillies with good intentions of throwing them into stir-fries, scattering them over noodles, and giving heat to curries, but always struggle to use up the last few. This Thai-style sweet chilli sauce is excellent for dipping, adding to dressings and, of course, gifting to a loved one.

TIP Chillies vary in heat intensity. Remove the seeds and pith if you want a milder sauce, or leave them in for a hotter experience.

3 red chillies

4 cloves of garlic, peeled

Small handful of coriander (cilantro) leaves

Zest of 1 unwaxed lime

200g (7oz/1 cup) sugar

1 rounded tbsp cornflour (cornstarch)

100ml (3½fl oz/scant ½ cup) white wine vinegar

Blitz the chillies, garlic, coriander and lime zest in a food processor, or finely chop and combine.

Add the chilli mix to a frying pan with the sugar, cornflour and 250ml (8¾fl oz/1 cup) of cold water. Bring to the boil over a high heat, then reduce to a simmer for 10 minutes, stirring frequently.

Pour in the vinegar and simmer the sauce for a further 3 minutes. Allow to cool, then pour into a clean, airtight jar.

spicy peanut sauce

Serves 4

No Thai-style feast would be complete without a spicy peanut sauce. Spoon over noodles or simply serve as a dip for guests to tuck into.

TIP Add more or fewer chilli flakes to suit your taste.

2 tsp sunflower oil

Pinch of dried chilli flakes (red pepper flakes)

4 rounded tbsp smooth peanut butter

1 spring onion (scallion), finely chopped

1 tbsp dark soy sauce

Heat the oil in a frying pan and add the chilli flakes. Infuse over a medium–high heat for 1–2 minutes.

Reduce the heat to low–medium and spoon in the peanut butter. Pour in 100ml (3½fl oz/scant ½ cup) cold water and use a balloon whisk to beat until smooth.

Stir through the spring onion and soy sauce.

lime and chive salad dressing

Serves 2

This zesty salad dressing is so simple to make and it works well with various salads, especially those with a spicy edge to them.

─────

TIP Switch chives for fresh coriander (cilantro) for an easy flavour variation.

6 tbsp good-quality extra virgin olive oil

1 unwaxed lime

Handful of chives, finely chopped

Pinch of freshly ground black pepper

Spoon the oil into a lidded jar.

Finely grate the zest of the lime into the jar, then halve the lime and squeeze in the juice through a sieve.

Add the chives to the jar. Secure the lid and shake until combined, then season with black pepper.

cupboard-raid sandwich spread

Serves 4 generously

I always have a jar of this budget-friendly sandwich spread ready for creating tasty sandwiches. I love mine spread thickly, then loaded with rocket (arugula) and olives. The beauty of this simple spread is that you can add the extras you have available, from a handful of flat-leaf parsley to sundried tomatoes, or perhaps a drizzle of chilli oil.

TIP Cooking the lentils in an 850W microwave is the key to the fast speed of this sandwich spread, but if you don't have a microwave, you can cook the lentils and stock in a pan for 25 minutes, over a medium heat.

150g (5½oz/scant 1 cup) dried red lentils, rinsed

600ml (20fl oz/2½ cups) hot vegetable stock

Drizzle of extra virgin olive oil

Juice of ¼ unwaxed lemon

Generous pinch of sea salt

Add the red lentils and 500ml (17½fl oz/2 cups) of the hot stock to a heatproof bowl and cook in a microwave for 14 minutes, stirring halfway through the cooking time.

Carefully remove from the microwave, then pour in the remaining 100ml (3½fl oz/ scant ½ cup) of vegetable stock. Use a fork to gently mash down the lentils. Stir in the oil and lemon juice and season with sea salt.

Allow to cool, then keep refrigerated in an airtight jar for up to 3 days.

roasted tomato and rosemary sauce

Serves 2

Sweet plum tomatoes and woody rosemary are a beautiful flavour marriage. Use this sauce to stir through pasta, add to a pizza or drizzle over Mediterranean vegetables.

TIP This is a great way to use up leftover tomatoes at the end of the week.

300g (10½oz) baby plum tomatoes

1 onion, roughly chopped

1 clove of garlic, peeled

½ tsp dried rosemary

Drizzle of olive oil, for roasting

50ml (1¾fl oz/scant ¼ cup) good-quality extra virgin olive oil

Pinch of sea salt and freshly ground black pepper

Preheat the oven to 200°C/400°F/Gas 6.

Arrange the whole tomatoes on a baking tray. Add the onion and whole garlic clove to the tray and sprinkle with the rosemary. Drizzle with olive oil, then roast for 12–13 minutes until the tomatoes have softened.

Spoon the tomatoes, onion and garlic into a blender. Pour in the extra virgin olive oil and blend on a high setting until smooth and creamy. Season the sauce with salt and black pepper.

ten-minute perfect pasta sauce

Serves 4

Tomato pasta can be all you need for a good meal. This homemade sauce is tastier than a jar of store-bought sauce. Make in bulk and freeze for easy weekday meals.

———————

TIP Freeze in portion-sized tubs or bags so they are ready to defrost when you need them, with no waste.

1 tbsp sunflower oil

2 cloves of garlic, peeled and crushed

½ tsp dried chilli flakes (red pepper flakes); optional

400g (14oz/1½ cups) passata (strained tomatoes)

½ tsp granulated sugar

Generous pinch of sea salt flakes and freshly ground black pepper

Heat the oil in a saucepan over a medium heat and cook the garlic for 1 minute until softened, then add the chilli flakes and cook for a further minute, stirring to avoid sticking. (The addition of dried chilli flakes gives a little heat to this sauce, but it is also delicious without.)

Stir in the passata and sugar, then simmer for 10 minutes.

Remove from the heat and season well with sea salt and black pepper.

index

about the author

Katy Beskow is an award-winning cook, writer and cookery tutor with a passion for seasonal ingredients, vibrant food and fuss-free home cooking. Once inspired by a bustling and colourful fruit and veg market in South London, Katy now lives in rural Yorkshire and cooks from a small (yet perfectly functioning) kitchen. She blogs at **www.katybeskow.com**.

Katy is the author of *15-Minute Vegan* (2017), *15-Minute Vegan Comfort Food* (2018), *15-Minute Vegan on a Budget* (2019), *Five Ingredient Vegan* (2019), *Vegan Fakeaway* (2020), *Easy Vegan Bible* (2020), *Vegan Roasting Pan* (2021), *Vegan BBQ* (2022), *Easy Speedy Vegan* (2022) and *Easy Vegan Christmas* (2023). This is her eleventh book, which combines all her favourite recipes from the original *15-Minute Vegan* trilogy.

Managing director: Sarah Lavelle

Editors: Romilly Morgan, Zena Alkayat, Harriet Webster and Sofie Shearman

Design: Gemma Hayden

Photography: Dan Jones

Photographer's assistant: Aloha Bonser Shaw

Food and prop stylist: Emily Ezekiel

Food stylist's assistants: Anna Barnett and Kitty Coles

Production: Tom Moore, Vincent Smith, Nikolaus Ginelli, Sabeena Atchia, Stephen Lang

Photography and text extracted from *15-Minute Vegan*, *15-Minute Vegan Comfort Food* and *15-Minute Vegan on a Budget* – first published in 2017, 2018 and 2019 (respectively) by Quadrille, an imprint of Hardie Grant Publishing.

This revised edition first published in 2023.

Quadrille

52–54 Southwark Street

London SE1 1UN

quadrille.com

Cataloguing in Publication Data: a catalogue record for this book is available from the British Library.

Text © 2023 Katy Beskow
Photography © 2023 Dan Jones
Author image page 318 © 2023 Luke Albert
Design and layout © 2023 Quadrille Publishing

ISBN: 9781837830374

Printed in China